# Abstract film and beyond

Malcolm Le Grice

# Abstract film and beyond

The MIT Press
Cambridge, Massachusetts, and London, England

*For Judith*

First paperback edition, 1981
First MIT Press edition, 1977

First published in Great Britain
by Studio Vista Publishers
and copyright © Malcolm Le Grice, 1977

Library of Congress catalog card number: 76-51506
ISBN 0-262-12077-1 (hard)
      0-262-62038-3 (paper)

Printed and bound in the United States of America

# Contents

**Acknowledgments**

I am very grateful to the following for openly sharing ideas, research and stills: David Curtis, Peter Gidal, Birgit and Wilhelm Hein, Helge Krarup, Katrina Martin, Louise O'Konor and particularly William Moritz, who gave me access to all his lengthy work on Oskar Fischinger before publication fully aware that I might be the first to present some of the information contained therein. I offer thanks to the Museum of Modern Art (New York) for study facilities and access to their film archive and to the following for the supply of stills for publication: the Arts Council of Great Britain, Peter Bloch, Simon Field, the Eggeling family, Elfriede Fischinger, the National Museum of Wales, the London Filmmakers Co-operative, the Nationalmuseum Stockholm and all the individual filmmakers who provided pictures of their own work. For assistance in the preparation of the manuscript or illustrations I wish to thank Tim Cawkwell, David Crosswaite, Esther Eisenthal, Sam Hughes and Glenys Kelly. *Rotary demi-sphere* (p. 42) is reproduced by permission of Trianon Press. *Ballet Mécanique* (pp. 37, 39, 41) is reproduced by permission of S.P.A.D.E.M., © S.P.A.D.E.M., Paris 1976. The illustration on p. 49 is reproduced by kind permission of Lund Humphries. The illustrations on pp. 9, 11, 15 and 76 appear by kind permission of the Tate Gallery.

# 1 · Art and cinematography

*The Assassination of the Duke of Guise* was the first production of a company called Le Film d'art, which in 1908 tried to elevate the Kinematograph, a bastard of the circus and side-show, to the level of high art. The director, Le Bargy, and his company of actors from the Comédie-Française, tried to achieve this lofty purpose by the application of acting standards and techniques drawn from the bourgeois theatre of that time—and, incidentally, in that production, also by music specially composed by Saint-Saëns. There is nothing special about this obscure film except as a symbol of cinema's early wish to raise itself above the level of an amusing, technical novelty, but it is interesting that, though this film looks pompous, most attempts to develop film as art have followed the pattern which applies principles from the theatre or the novel. This dominance has become a deeply established norm. Popularly, no alternative is known. While films may be documentaries or fiction, their essential form and language has been evolved to tell stories.

There is no inevitability in cinema's history; it is the result of needs, priorities, social and economic pressures. In a theoretical sense, there is no reason why the plastic arts—painting and sculpture or music—should not have emerged as the dominant formal basis for cinematic culture. Indeed, given the particularly revolutionary developments which took place in the formal notions of those arts in the first twenty years or so of this century—the cinema's formative years—it is almost surprising that they did not have an overwhelming effect on the new medium. The surprise (I might almost say the sense of historical 'error') is increased when the effect of the new technological developments of photography and cinematography can be seen as significant influences on the plastic arts of that period. Some of the formal notions of painting at that time can be seen as intrinsically more 'cinematic' than anything which was achieved in cinema as such. From Manet and Degas and the Impressionists proper, the influence and importance of photography is acknowledged. The search for an empirical basis for their work, opposed to the symbolic contrivance of 'history' and 'subject' painting, not only contributed to the philosophical shift of the nineteenth century but also to the inquisitiveness which had led to the invention of the photographic process.

Impressionism with its high point in Monet can be well represented by his Rouen Cathedral series. This series of over twenty paintings is mostly of the cathedral's façade from the same viewpoint—reputedly from a room above a shop called 'Au Caprice', the name being ironic, as the difficult and intense project took two years from February 1892 to complete. Focus on the effects of different lighting conditions, at different times of day, was made possible by the consistent 'subject matter'. We are accustomed to photographic emulsions which respond to light extremely quickly, so we tend not to consider exposure as other than a fraction of a second—a 'snap' rather than a process. In truth, by 1877 emulsions were already 'fast' enough for Muybridge to photograph

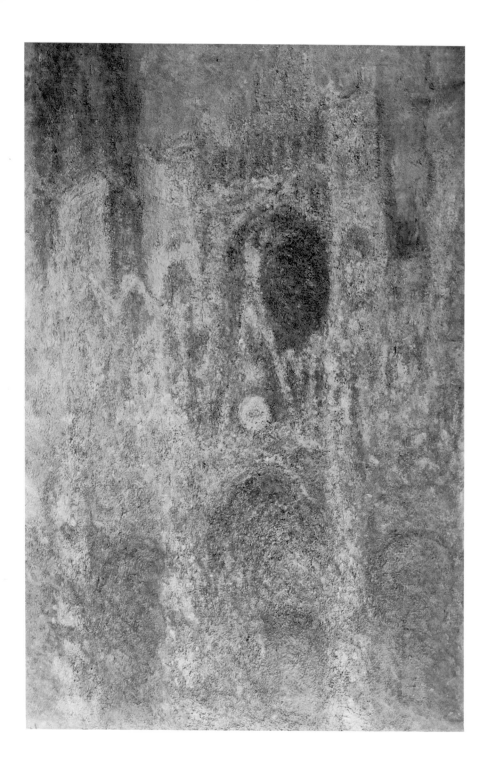

Paul Cézanne: *Still Life with Water Jug*, 1892–3

*left*
Claude Monet: *Rouen Cathedral: the Façade in Sunlight*, 1894

'"Occident" . . . trotting past me at the rate of 2.27, accurately timed
. . . the exposure . . . being less than 1/1000 of a second'. But Beaumont
Newhall's *History of Photography*, mentions that 'one "victim" re-
collected that in 1840 he sat in a Daguerrotype portrait gallery for eight
minutes with the strong sunlight shining on his face and tears trickling
down his cheeks, while the operator promenaded the room with watch
in hand, calling out the time every five seconds, till the fountains of his
eyes were dry'. Thus Monet's process can be thought of as somewhat
analogous to that of photography. And the single brushmark style of
Monet and the other Impressionists could even be compared with the
'grain' of a photographic image.

Whatever the obvious similarities between Impressionism and the
photographic process, the most significant parallel lies at the more
fundamental, philosophical level. The nineteenth century saw the decline
of a religious view of the world, with its basis in faith and underlying
quietism, replaced by a scientific materialism, with its basis in observation, experiment and technological determination. Photography was a
result of this philosophical transition, and, as an observational instrument, still significantly aids scientific research. The Impressionist painters
subscribed to the scientific view by their establishment of an art form
based on the recording of observation. But in an Impressionist painting,
the subject of the observation is not simply, for example, the light falling
on Rouen Cathedral. Both the material constraints of painting—colour,
pigment, canvas—and the artist as a perceiver and organizer of his

sensations significantly effect the 'impression' which is the residue of his labour. If not totally clear in Monet, this is certainly evident in the paintings of Paul Cézanne. Cézanne is rightly spoken of as a Post-Impressionist in as far as his work is firmly based on observation. However where the assumed 'aim' of the Impressionist was the recording of the artist's visual impression of the world, Cézanne became increasingly aware that the 'appearance' of the world was something constructed from the activity of the observer. All manner of factors conditioned his experience, particularly the established pictorial conventions inherited from his culture, which he had to modify in order to make new perception possible. He also realized that the material and process of painting significantly conditioned perception, and Cézanne, through the works themselves, more than any other artist of his period, does most to create an awareness of the 'relativistic' nature of perception. Cézanne becomes, and makes us, aware of the flux of perception through process. And being concerned with 'process' does most to introduce the time factor into painting—not simply the time it takes to make the picture, but awareness of the way in which perception changes through the production of the work. A line from Cézanne to the analytical Cubism of Picasso and Braque, is frequently drawn, and was largely understood and acknowledged by the artists themselves. It traces a progressive dissolution of 'external' objects as entities separate from their surrounding space, or perceivable independently of the act of painting, perceiving, reorganizing and comprehending; in short, objects come to be seen as inseparable from the complex time–space processes of which they are part.

It is at this point, both in terms of the historical period—the first decade or so of the twentieth century—and in terms of the formal innovations in painting, where the most clear relationships can be drawn with the medium of film. In the same way in which the nineteenth-century artists had been influenced by photography, the artists of the early part of this century were excited by cinematography, which influenced the form of their current work and led increasingly to a wish to make use of the new medium.

Of the many art movements of this early period, it is perhaps not surprising that the Futurists considered cinema most consistently. The movement was widespread, being particularly strong in Italy and Russia, and, like Dada, Futurism was a broad art movement or philosophy, not confined to a specific medium. Its ideas and realized works ranged through painting, sculpture, music, theatre, poetry and film. To many Futurists, cinematography appeared as the most advanced medium for art, in which time, movement, mechanical image, electric light and, potentially, sound could fuse into a thoroughly twentieth-century experience. On 11 September 1916, Marinetti, Bruno Corra, Emilio Settimelli, Arnaldo Ginna, Giacomo Balla and Remo Chiti issued a manifesto, 'The Futurist Cinema',[1] from which the following comes:

At first look the cinema, born only a few years ago, may seem to be Futurist already, lacking a past and free from traditions. Actually, by appearing in the guise of theatre without words, it had inherited all the most traditional sweepings of the literary theatre. Consequently, everything we have said and done about the stage applies to the

Pablo Picasso: *Seated Nude*, 1909–10

cinema. Our action is legitimate and necessary in so far as the cinema up to now has been and tends to remain profoundly passéist, whereas we see in it the possibility of an eminently Futurist art and the expressive medium most adapted to the complex sensibility of a Futurist artist.

We can see in this passage an attempt to separate the still unexploited elements of cinematography from the direction cinema had already strongly established. Like the Dadaist movement, much of the energy of the Futurists was directed into attacking established aspects of culture, and they were particularly concerned about the 'misuse' of cinema as it had already contaminated the most ready-made Futurist medium. The same manifesto continues later:

The Cinema is an autonomous art. The cinema must therefore never copy the stage. The cinema, being essentially visual, must above all fulfil the evolution of painting, detach itself from reality, from photography, from the graceful and solemn. It must become anti-graceful, deforming, impressionistic, synthetic, dynamic, free-wording.

ONE MUST FREE THE CINEMA AS AN EXPRESSIVE MEDIUM in order to make it the ideal instrument of a new art, immensely vaster and lighter than all the existing arts. We are convinced that only in this way can one reach that polyexpressiveness toward which all the most modern artistic researches are moving. Today the Futurist cinema creates precisely the polyexpressive symphony which just a year ago we announced in our manifesto . . .

The final section of the manifesto is a list of fourteen positive directions which it sees as open to Futurist cinema, summing up as follows:

Painting + sculpture + plastic dynamism + words-in-freedom + composed noises + architecture + synthetic theatre = Futurist cinema.

THIS IS HOW WE DECOMPOSE AND RECOMPOSE THE UNIVERSE ACCORDING TO OUR MARVELLOUS WHIMS, to centuple the powers of the Italian creative genius and its absolute pre-eminence in the world.

In the light of recent historical information, there is a curious factor about the list of possibilities which appear in the manifesto. Except as an inference which can be drawn from the general tone of the writing and from its most generalized statements, nowhere does it explicitly visualize a non-representational, abstract cinema. What it does summon up is a cinematic form allied to that which stems from Dada or Surrealism, for example number nine of their list:

CONGRESSES, FLIRTS, FIGHTS AND MARRIAGES OF FUNNY FACES, MIMICRY, ETC. Example: a big nose that silences a thousand congressional fingers by ringing an ear, while two policemen's moustaches arrest a tooth.

Or number eleven:

FILMED DRAMAS OF DISPROPORTION (a thirsty man who pulls out a tiny drinking straw that lengthens umbilically as far as the lake and dries it up instantly).

This inattention to a non-representational cinema is all the more curious as Arnaldo Ginna and his brother, Bruno Corra, had already in

1912 written a detailed article (for a collection edited by Corra and Settimelli) titled 'Abstract Cinema, Chromatic Music', containing a detailed account of two years of experiment which gave rise to a number of realized film works. Though these films are not available for study (they probably no longer exist), the tone and detail of the 1912 article rings true, in which case they currently represent the first recorded, genuinely abstract films.

The 1916 manifesto was written at the time its authors were working on the film *Vita Futurista*. Though no copy of this long film now seems to exist, there is documentary evidence of its first public showing at the Niccolini Theatre in Florence on 28 January 1917. Information as to its contents also mostly stems from Ginna and a report in *Bianco e Nero* (May–June 1965). The descriptions are not only supported by surviving stills from various sections of the film, but the character of the scenario matches that of the proposals listed in the manifesto. For example, from a 1916 article in *L'Italia Futurista* one section of the film is summarized as follows: 'Balla falls in love with and marries a chair, a footstool is born.' Though another section of this film is called 'The dance of geometric splendour' there is no evidence that any section was conceived as strictly abstract. There can be little doubt that the film was a major work of the avant-garde cinema, and was genuinely representative of the Italian Futurists' contemporary view of film (in contrast to *Perfidio Incanto* more usually quoted in this context). There is also little doubt that formally it was allied closely to the later Dadaist and Surrealist works in cinema, being concerned both with attacking contemporary popular sensibility, and using representational situations in a dramatic and symbolist way—all of which places it, with *Perfidio Incanto*, essentially outside the scope of this book.[2]

Like Italian Futurism, its counterpart in Russia also had a significant effect on thinking about the form and role of cinema. But here, again, there are no surviving works from the early period which adequately represent this effect. In Russia the real influence of Futurist thinking on cinema, and, one might argue, its most adequate embodiment in formal terms anywhere, comes much later through Dziga Vertov, and specifically in *Man with the Movie Camera* (1929).

Though Marinetti visited Russia in 1914, the Russian Futurists were in many ways an independent movement and had already achieved one film, *Drama in the Futurists' Cabaret 13* (1913), made by the painters Burliuk, Larionov and Goncharova, and described by Jay Leyda in *Kino* as 'a parody on the prevalent genre of film-guignol'. The very young revolutionary poet, Vladimir Mayakovsky, had joined the Futurists in 1911 and continued to be an outspoken influence on artists in Russia until his suicide in 1930. He was always enthusiastic about the possibilities of a Futurist cinema, though he destroyed his earliest attempt at a scenario. He was outspoken on film matters throughout the post-Revolutionary reorganization of the film industry in Russia, and, whilst always frustrated in particular, his energy probably had a general influence on the subsequent organization. In 1918 he directed and starred in *The Young Lady and the Hooligan*, one of the first productions after the Revolution. The film is of little interest formally, though its story content is radical, a kind of precursor of *Rebel Without a Cause* with Mayakovsky as a slightly improbable James Dean.

Though not a Futurist, Kasimir Malevich almost certainly contemplated the production of a Suprematist film in the period just before the Revolution, although it is almost equally certain that the project was never realized.

At the turn of the century mechanized manufacture, vast increases in speed and travel, introduced experiences of changing perception at rates previously inconceivable. The result was a fragmentation of our experience, no longer dominated by the stability of a reassuring 'home base' as a centre for our perceptions and self-identification. It is clear that the growing predominance of simple geometric forms and angular planes in the art of this period reflects the exterior shape of the mechanical world. But there is also a clear trace of the artists' fascination with the dynamic problems of speed, change and fragmentation themselves, reflecting the new experience of travel and communication. As the rapid move away from figuration to abstraction in art went on, increasingly the interior relations of elements within the work were used to imply motion. Whereas work like that of Mondrian or van Doesburg, which had developed from Cézanne and the Cubists, mostly interprets its dynamic in terms of a new 'architectural' analogy, work like that of Kandinsky or Malevich, deriving from Futurism and Expressionism, tends towards a kinetic interpretation. I have already indicated that my view of the Cézanne–Cubist development is essentially concerned with its exploration of the dynamic of perception. While the *initial* process of pictorial fragmentation is a necessary common basis for both Futurist and Cubist work, there can be no doubt that the architectural synthesis is significantly different from the kinetic. Certainly artists of the time saw this difference as a major factor.

Bragaglia and Boccioni reacted against the lack of motion analysis in the cinematograph. In the pamphlet, 'Futurist photodynamism' (1911), Bragaglia says:

> Cinematography does not trace the shape of movement. It subdivides it, without rules, with mechanical arbitrariness, disintegrating and shattering it without any kind of aesthetic concern for rhythm . . . Besides which, cinematography never analyses movement. It shatters it in the frames of the film strip, quite unlike the action of photodynamism, which analyses movement precisely in its details. And cinematography never synthesizes movement, either. It merely reconstructs fragments of reality, already coldly broken up, in the same way as the hand of the chronometer deals with time even though this flows in a continuous and constant stream.

Though this statement seems to be 'against' film, in many ways it represents an understanding of the nature of the medium and its limits, even if it fails to visualize new creative possibilities for it. He goes on to level similar criticism at the chronophotography of Marey. Bragaglia's distinction between mechanical recording–reconstruction and analysis is enlightening, but I must attest to the obvious relationship between the motion photographs of Marey and Muybridge, and his own works as well as those of Balla, Boccioni, Carra and, of course, Duchamp. Not to see the relationship is perverse, and even in their paintings a direct experience of 'reconstructed' motion is possible from their motion

G. Severini: *Suburban Train arriving at Paris*, 1915

analysis. So, an experience of motion can occur, even without the discreet sequential re-presentation of the cinematograph, and it is at this point that the combination of abstraction and a kinetic dynamic begins to emerge.

I have considered the progressive dissolution of the pictorial form of perceived reality as it occurred through Impressionism, Cézanne, Cubism and Futurism, and the synthetic aspect of reforming new representational space. However, there was an unpredictable development: through the fragmentation of representational space, and increased concern for the dynamic relationship of objects, it emerged that the painterly means used to 'describe' these relationships could be separated from any representational function. Though non-representational in the pictorial sense, abstract work is not necessarily non-referential. Just to counteract the myths which derive basically from the 'L'art pour l'art' slogan of that period, abstraction does not 'free' art from relatability to 'life', it merely alters the regions of experience which can be dealt with and the kinds of relationship which are possible. In particular abstraction opens up two significant possibilities: the first stems from considering painterly form as diagrammatic rather than pictorial representation, the second from direct perceptual response to the material and form of the work as an object itself. The ramifications of this, as a good fifty years of continuing exploration have shown, were extensive. Art, instead of representing the world, could now be a model for it, functioning as analogy rather than imitation. In addition artists could explore regions of perceptual experience which could only be the product of the special nature of the medium in question, in no way available in the world except as created through art.

Whatever the subsequent development of abstract art, much of the earliest work and what is of most interest in relation to film, is concerned with motion and transformation. In the same way in which when viewing a Marey chronophotograph the eye shifts from trace to trace of the figure and reconstructs the movement, the abstraction of this, for example in Gino Severini's *Suburban Train arriving at Paris* (1915) or Duchamp's *Nude Descending a Staircase* pictures (1911 and 1912), began to show how the kinetic experience was not specifically tied to the representational elements of the image. The repetition of similar forms in close proximity allowed the eye to 'flicker' from one to the other, interpreting them as the same 'object' in different positions in time, as opposed to different objects in a space. The artists whose abstract work has most in common with the aims inherent in the early film movement were all Russian—Wassily Kandinsky, usually credited with the earliest abstract work in 1910; Kasimir Malevich, initiator of Suprematism; and El Lissitzky—though after 1915 other artists began to explore the possibilities of motion and transformation using simplified geometric forms, including Hans Arp and two of the artists who contributed directly to abstract film, Eggeling and Richter.

It is impossible here to search in detail for the parallels in the other media, but in literature there is the emergence of Dadaist poetry which challenged traditional syntax, logic, and habitual semantic relationships, leading to the Surrealist writing of Breton and thence the structure of *Finnegans Wake* by James Joyce. In music, it is possible to see the first stages of a similar process in the whole tone innovation of Debussy, culminating in the final dissolution of conventional harmony with its hierarchic intervals by the twelve-tone and note-row techniques of Schönberg. It is curious how some form of 'equalization of values' is common in the fragmentation texture of Cubist and Futurist painting, Joycean syntax and Schönberg's twelve-tone scale; is it only a poetic analogy to see some similarity with the mechanical stream of frames each one recorded with equal value by the cinematograph?

## 2 · The first abstract films

Though there has been some confusion and there may be some surprises in store, it now seems fairly certain that not only were the films made by Bruno Corra and Arnaldo Ginna, between 1910 and 1912, the first abstract films, but that they were probably the first avant-garde works of cinema of any kind. It seems unlikely that any copies of the films survive —they were all hand-made on clear celluloid, and as there was no form of colour film copying until the thirties the likelihood of the originals remaining in copyable state until then is extremely remote. However, Bruno Corra's document 'Abstract Cinema—Chromatic Music',[1] published in 1912, is both factual and convincing in its description of their work in film to that date. The title 'Chromatic Music' introduces a recurring tendency of artists concerned with abstract film to pursue a musical analogy for their work. It is difficult to think of music, certainly instrumental music, as ever having been other than essentially abstract, and considering that film like music is a time-based medium, it is not surprising that the analogy with music should be used, and that this analogy should continue to effect contemporary abstract film-makers.

In his article Corra argues that the chromatic scale consists of only one octave, on the assumption that the eye, unlike the ear, lacks the power of resolution—by which he means either that the eye does not appreciate an equivalent to the harmonic resolution of a key in music, or more simply (but less likely) that it lacks the discrimination of precise interval. He says:

> Yet we felt the obvious need of a subdivision of the solar spectrum, even an artificial and arbitrary one (since the effect stems principally from the *relationships* between the colours that impress the eye). Consequently we selected four equally distanced gradations in each colour. We had four reds chosen at equal distances in the spectrum, four greens, four violets etc. In this way we managed to extend the seven colours in four octaves. After the violet of the first octave came the red of the second, and so on. To translate all this into practice we naturally used a series of twenty-eight coloured electric light bulbs, corresponding to twenty-eight keys. Each bulb was fitted with an oblong reflector: the first experiments were done with direct light, and in subsequent ones a sheet of ground glass was placed in front of the light bulb. The key board was exactly like that of a piano (but was less extensive). When an octave was played for example, the two colours were mingled, as are two sounds on the piano.

The production of this 'colour-organ' introduces another element which has a general place in the development of abstract cinema. As early as 1880 in America, Bainbridge Bishop and, soon afterwards, Wallace Rimington, constructed colour-organs. The beginning of this concept, though, can be placed much earlier, at least as early as 1734 with the Clavecin Oculaire of Louis-Bertrand Castel. In fact, experimenters in this field in and around the end of the nineteenth century would make quite a considerable list. Extensions of the idea persist to

in particular had taken. Hans Richter writes:

Problems in modern art lead directly into the film. Organization and orchestration of form, color, the dynamics of motion, simultaneity, were problems with which Cézanne, the Cubists and Futurists had to deal. Eggeling and I came directly out of the structural problems of abstract art *nolens volens* into the film medium. The connection to theatre and literature was completely severed. Cubism, Expressionism, Dadaism, abstract art, Surrealism found not only their expression in films, but a new fulfilment on a new level.[3]

It is difficult to imagine that most artists at that time did not talk about the possibilities for film, and many must have contemplated using it. However, the movement to film in the cases of Richter and Eggeling was particularly logical and an organic development of their drawing and painting, which they extended into scroll form. Both had been for many years involved in the problems of modern art, had travelled widely in Europe and become involved in the debates and activities of groups like the Dadaists. For them, film was an extension of their art activity and its background philosophy.

Ruttmann was of a similar age (all three were born in the 1880s), had been trained as an architect and studied painting from 1909 in Munich. He became interested in the new abstract tendency, but there is no evidence that he ever became deeply involved in the philosophical problems of art. I do not know the nature of the paintings prior to his film work, and he certainly seems to have made no impact as a painter on his contemporaries.

Oskar Fischinger, born in 1900, was some thirteen years younger than Ruttmann and only twenty-one when they first met in Frankfurt, the occasion of the first screening of Ruttmann's *Opus 1*. Though he had already worked as a draughtsman and was deeply interested in music, becoming apprentice to an organ-maker on leaving school, his first work as an artist was in the film medium.

Were these four a 'group'? In the strict sense they were not. They knew of each other's work: for a time Eggeling and Richter worked extremely closely together, while Ruttmann and Fischinger corresponded—there is even some suggestion that Fischinger may have assisted Ruttmann on some productions and he certainly sold Ruttmann a piece of animation equipment which he had invented. The collaboration between Eggeling and Richter was based on artistic theory; that between Ruttmann and Fischinger much more on technical grounds, though curiously their work is more similar.

Much has been made of the collaboration between Eggeling and Richter, and certainly between 1919 and 1921 the two artists spent a considerable amount of time together, living at the Richter family home in Klein-Kölzig about seventy miles from Berlin. From the evidence of their respective work prior to this period, I would consider Eggeling to have been the more advanced artist, clearer about his intentions, and the nature of his artistic problems. Where Richter's energy had been focused outside his individual works in the movements which surrounded him, Eggeling had concentrated consistently on the direct artistic problems of his drawing and painting. Richter has described his impression of Eggeling after Tristan Tzara had introduced them in 1918 in Zurich:

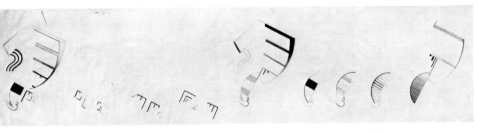

Viking Eggeling: *Diagonal Symphony.* Scroll drawing completed between 1921 and 1925

> Eggeling had succeeded in articulating a complete syntax of form-relationships which he called 'Generalbass der Malerei' or 'Bass Motif of Painting' . . . He had been preparing himself by his 'Elementary Tablets' and his 'Orchestration of Line'. On the basis of polar relationships, by the interplay of contrasts and analogies, an unlimited vocabulary developed: a vertical line was accentuated by a horizontal, a strong line contrasted with a weak one, a single line gained importance from many lines and so on . . . His didactic qualities led to a new understanding of the elements of expression. He became an artist of a special kind in a special way.
>
> I profitted enormously from his experience. He was far ahead of me. On the other hand he needed my spontaneity.[4]

Eggeling, like other artists who had dispensed with representation, and who saw the visual elements of line, shape and colour as free from a visual imitative function, sought another 'rationale'. He saw in music a logical basis for composition within an abstract medium and that visual forms could similarly be susceptible to laws of composition, at the same time providing the basis of a universal language. Eggeling's theoretical writing, like Kandinsky's in *Concerning the Spiritual in Art* (written in 1910), includes a strong metaphysical component. In an article which he wrote for the magazine *MA* in 1921, titled 'Theoretical presentations of the art of movement', he found it necessary to distinguish between a 'transcendental' and 'practical' definition for art. In its transcendental aspect he saw art as an expression of a striving for greater perfection, the search for a higher unity of man in mankind. He considered that man's awareness of this potential rested on insight. In its practical aspect he sought primarily a strict economy of means, and 'a strict discipline of the elements'. 'Art is not the subjective explosion of the individual, but becomes the organic language of mankind, which must be basically free of misconceptions, clear-cut, so that it can become a vehicle for communication.'

Eggeling's development as an artist had been essentially from the position of a landscape painter, greatly influenced by Cézanne. His progression had been through a greater and greater economy, gradually eliminating all but that which could be achieved through a series of simple and definable elements of line, curve and elementary shade. The units of the drawing itself gradually superseded the landscape in order of importance, until by 1919 no trace of direct external reference remained.

Eggeling's 1919 article for *MA* was accompanied by four drawings from his developmental series, *Horizontal-Vertical Orchestra*, his major work of that time. In 1920 Eggeling and Richter applied to UFA in Berlin (Universum-Film-Aktiengesellschaft, a state-aided film production company), for support to carry out a film project. Though it is contended by Richter, I consider that, from the evidence presented by Louise O'Konor, the basis of this early film project was most probably *Horizontal-Vertical Orchestra*. In 1921, following a visit to Richter and Eggeling at Klein-Kölzig, Theo van Doesburg wrote of their film experiments:

The drawings needed for the mechanical production of a composition consist of long scrolls serving as a score in which the development of the composition is set down in a consecutive arrangement, but so that the intervening gaps are developed mechanically. [This is unclear, but most probably it meant that each of the intervening stages was drawn step by step, though this may have been left to an animation artist at UFA.] These precisely executed drawings, in black, white, and grey, in spite of their careful execution, were still found to lack precision . . . The first experiments to be shown were confined to compositions in black, white, and grey; the reproduction found in this issue [*Horizontal-Vertical Orchestra III* scroll] gives a rough impression of such a composition at the moment that a particular sequence has reached its pitch through the effect of lighting. This 'central part' is then gradually developed again until the arrangement has reached a total visual entity. Thus this reproduction presents no more than one particular point of one particular arrangement in the composition, but can in fact not be dissociated from the movement provided by the lighting mechanism [what is meant by this is unclear] of film.[5]

Whether the film described by van Doesburg was *Horizontal-Vertical Orchestra* or not, Eggeling's only surviving film is called *Diagonal Symphony* and is based on the scroll work of that name. Aspects of the description, particularly those concerned with lighting effects and the inclusion of a grey aspect—*Diagonal Symphony* entirely composed of white forms on black—suggest that it is not the surviving film, and the description of the forms rules out the possibility that the film was Richter's *Rhythmus 21*.

Eggeling and Richter ceased their collaboration under a cloud somewhere around the end of 1921; Eggeling moved to Berlin and set up a studio. In the summer of 1922 he visited his sister in Sweden, borrowed money for a camera and projector, and constructed a primitive animation table. It is likely that Eggeling continued work on a film version of *Horizontal-Vertical Orchestra*, beginning *Diagonal Symphony* in the summer of 1923, and showing the completed film to artist friends, including Moholy-Nagy, on 5 November 1924. The date is recorded in a review by critic Paul Schmidt,[6] though again no precise title for the film is given. The film received its first public presentation in Berlin on 3 May 1925, this time clearly named *Diagonal Symphony*, together with Hirschfeld-Mack's light projections from the Bauhaus (*Dreiteilige Farbensonatine, Reflektorische Farbenspiel*), Richter's *Film ist Rhythmus*, Ruttmann's *Opus 2, 3* and *4*, Fernand Léger and Dudley Murphy's *Images Mobiles* (all or part of *Ballet Mécanique*), and René Clair's *Entr'acte* (from a scenario by Francis Picabia). Eggeling died sixteen days later.

The surviving version of *Diagonal Symphony*, which is nearly eight

Viking Eggeling: *Diagonal Symphony*. Film completed
between 1921 and 1925

minutes long, may be incomplete or changed from the original but it is fortunately in excellent condition and is more than adequate as a representation of the film's intentions. It is essentially composed of a series of developments of white abstract figures on a black ground. All the figures are centrally placed, and there is no movement across the frame in any direction, nor is there any spatial factor created by diminishing or enlarging the figure. In other words, all attention is drawn to the transformations which take place within the figures, as far as possible isolated within a neutral frame. Though some of the lines are thicker than others, and approach 'blocked-in' shapes, the figures are almost entirely composed of simple linear elements. The combinations and transformations are always additive: the complex figures are composed of built-up elements, and having been established do not alter their form. In some cases, whole figures may be reversed through a vertical or horizontal axis, all basic topological transformations. The rules of development, like the elements and figures themselves, are extremely simple and consistent with Eggeling's intention to build a language from basic elements. Eggeling thought of his work as more than individual-istic, as a first step in the development of a precise visual language. The animation style is extremely static. Nowhere, unlike his contemporaries, does he take his inspiration from the inventive possibilities of the medium and animation technique; his ideas remain consistent with his earlier development as an artist. He utilizes the medium, but does not explore it, and his work certainly does not express the dynamic factors of the age as visualized by the Futurists. The kinetic aspect is extremely muted, the movements being slow enough to be appreciated by the intellect as a series of transformations, rather than with a bodily kinetic empathy. Though he spoke of his language as being 'organic', it is 'organizational'—a treatise in visual logic, or a formal visual poem where the lines rhyme. The essential quality transmitted from the work is that of an austere integrity, and the principles of his film seem to have most in common with programmed, systematic and conceptual art of a more recent period.

Hans Richter was a many-faceted figure in the field of film and art in general. Not only was he a practising artist, but he was always involved in the general issues of art, particularly in the political sense. He was also one of those artists who fled Europe between the wars for political reasons, making his home in the USA, and at the same time forming a link between post-war European and American art. In particular, he was a major figure in stimulating interest in avant-garde cinema, and play-ing a significant role in the emergence of the post-war experimental film movement in America. He has been a teacher and writer on film, and has written a book on the Dada movement in art. Not only has most of the historical information about his own work reached us through him, but for a long time he has been the major source for information about the German developments in abstract cinema.
    From my own experience it is difficult to remember the precise sequence of events in one's own work, and it is not surprising that doubt has been cast by recent research on the assumed sequence of events in the period in question, including Richter's own early film work. I am not convinced that the current copies of *Rhythmus 21* and *Rhythmus 23* are

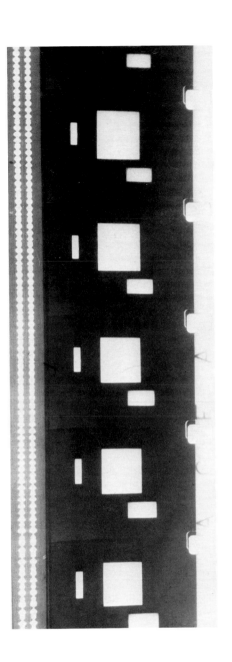

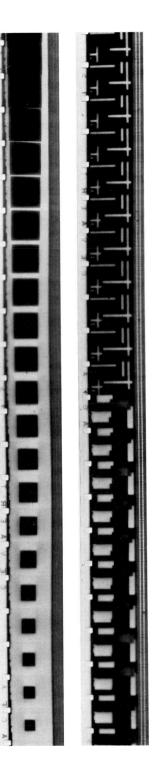

Hans Richter: *Rhythmus 23*,
1923

in their original form. They certainly did not have sound tracks as they do now and were possibly re-edited to some extent when they were compiled by Richter into *40 years of Experiment in Film*. But they do serve to represent his work of that period.

What of the works themselves? Of all the surviving films of that period, these two from Richter are technically the crudest. At the same time their simplicity allows certain basic factors to emerge in a way in which they do not in the films of his contemporaries. As Richter describes, they comprise mainly cut-out rectangles and squares of various sizes and tones. These are simply animated in a strong kinetic way, using movement in any direction, and particularly exploring a depth factor by having a square, for example, recede or rush outwards. His abstract films, unlike Eggeling's, embody the physical rhythms of movements in space. He has a bold awareness of the film's rectangle, sometimes changing the screen from white to black with broad diagonal sweeps. His 'surrender' to the technical difficulties of the medium allows his films to express some of the fundamental dynamic qualities inherent in rapid changes of shape and the simultaneous presentation of elements moving at different speeds. Though his forms come directly from the constructivist or suprematist movements in painting, his filmic abstraction is not so dominated by abstract painting as that of Eggeling. It points the way to an abstraction more related to cinema, and derived from its technology. Its simplicity of form accentuates the rhythmic experience, as Richter later indicates:

> When I say there is no *Form* in *Rhythm 21*, I mean that by taking the whole movie screen, pressing it together and opening it up, top, bottom, sides, right, left, you don't perceive form anymore, you perceive movement. From such an elementary demonstration I went on to take parts of the rectangular screen and move these *parts* together or against each other. These rectangles are not *forms*, they are parts of movement. The definition of form refers to one's perception of the formal quality of a single object, or several single objects; but, when you repeat this same form over and over again and in different positions, then the relationship between the positions becomes the thing to be perceived, not the single or individual form. One doesn't see the form or object anymore but rather the *relationship*. In this way you see a kind of rhythm.[7]

Next in the chronology of Richter's films is *Rhythmus 25*, of which there is no copy to my knowledge. Richter has described it as a hand-painted film in colour, while an illustration in *Hans Richter* entitled 'Study for *Rhythm 25*' shows it to continue the exploration of large simple geometric forms and subdivisions of the screen. His next film, *Film Study*, dated 1926, leaves me in much less doubt about the current copy's authenticity. Since its inclusion of live-action material arouses problems more related to the work which I shall deal with in the next chapter, I shall take it up again then.

If there is some doubt about the dating of the early works of Richter and Eggeling, there is no doubt about when Ruttmann showed his first film, *Lichtspiel Opus 1*. After a private presentation in Frankfurt in April 1921, which had been reported in the *Frankfurter Zeitung* of 2 April by Bernhard Diebold (a critic who had already done much to stimulate interest in the possibility of an abstract cinema), the same film was then shown publicly at the Marmorhaus in Berlin on the 27th of that month. The presentation was clearly a spectacular occasion, as the film was not only in colour, but was accompanied by live music especially composed by Swedish composer Max Butting. No copy of this film seems to have survived, but the original score for the music still exists, which includes drawings of the various motifs and their movement as part of the players' guide for synchronization. The formal notions and visual motives are similar to those of *Opus II*, the earliest surviving film.

As all the remaining films in the *Lichtspiel* series, *Opus II*, *III* and *IV*, are also coloured, it is probable that the manner of the colouring was similar in the first film. By modern standards, the coloured version which I have seen is not staggeringly bright, in fact no more than a single all-over, background toning of what would otherwise be the white areas of a black and white film, the figures remaining black. It is an overall tinting rather than a selective colouring. The background colour changes quite frequently in order to maintain interest in the colour factor. I think it most likely that the prints were made onto various lengths of coloured nitrate stock and the sections later spliced together, but Ruttmann may have done additional work by hand on the earliest prints which he made. The remaining films in the series were all premièred in Berlin on 25 June 1925, and were similarly accompanied by Butting's music. (It is possible, however, that *Opus IV* did not have its première until 1927 in Baden-Baden.)

The three sections which survive of the *Lichtspiel* series not only show an accomplished technical mastery and an assured orchestration of form, but also a distinct aesthetic development through the series. The first two films seem to have been the result of painting onto glass, a shape being able to grow in one direction whilst its trace is removed or modified in the other. They contain distinct tonal differentiation and a texture which could have been made by brush marks, or the effect may have been achieved by working in charcoal on paper. Yet, although impressed by this technical mastery, Richter was critical of Ruttmann's experiments at the artistic level: 'There was nothing of an articulate language (which was for us . . . the one and only reason to use this suspicious medium, film). It seemed to us "vieux Jeu", pure impressionism!'[8] In terms of the 'hard' theoretical approach of Eggeling, this criticism has some foundation, for Ruttmann was no art theorist. He took his inspiration from the medium and the new possibilities he was discovering through his own animation techniques. But then is this not equally true of Richter's films? At an aesthetic level, what Richter misses in Ruttmann's work is quite a highly developed musical form. This lies not only in the rhythm and pace of the forms themselves, as they grow, move and transform, but the sequences themselves repeat, as melodic units in a musical structure. The discipline of working with a composer to create a strictly timed accompaniment may have assisted the development of this sensibility in Ruttmann.

As the series progresses there is a gradual shift away from anthropomorphic interpretation of forms and their movement through a machine analogy towards more geometric form and finally the beginning of a more purely optical mode.

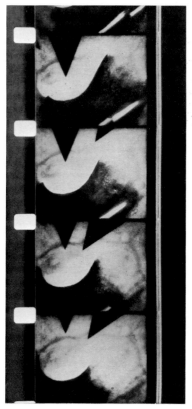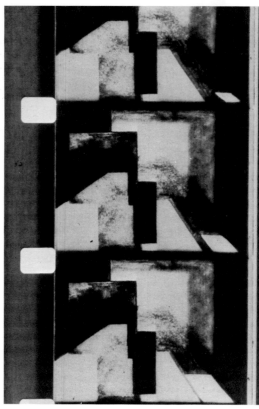

Walter Ruttmann: *Opus II*, 1921    *Opus III*, completed between 1922 and 1925
*right*
Walter Ruttmann: *Opus IV*, completed between 1923 and 1927

*Opus II* could be crudely characterized as being a battle between the
circle or soft, gently moving curved forms, and aggressively stabbing
black triangles, which mostly enter from above, chasing the softer forms.
Like much of Fischinger's music-based studies, the forms encourage
anthropomorphic interpretation, and the dance-like movements are
experienced by kinetic empathy.

In *Opus III* the triangles are mostly replaced by blunt pumping rectangles, which still force back and reform the softer shapes, though at
one stage these rectilinear forms emerge within a crescent and are
softened by it. As the film progresses, the concern is more and more with
the interaction of geometric forms, squares, rectangles, and later
parallelograms, on the diagonals from the lower corners of the frame.
The motion then becomes more machine-like—the forms act like
pistons, pumping in organic, 'heartbeat' rhythms. Finally the circle reappears and transforms the rectangles to large sweeping curves, but now
geometric rather than organic, which form the basis of the transformations to the end of the film.

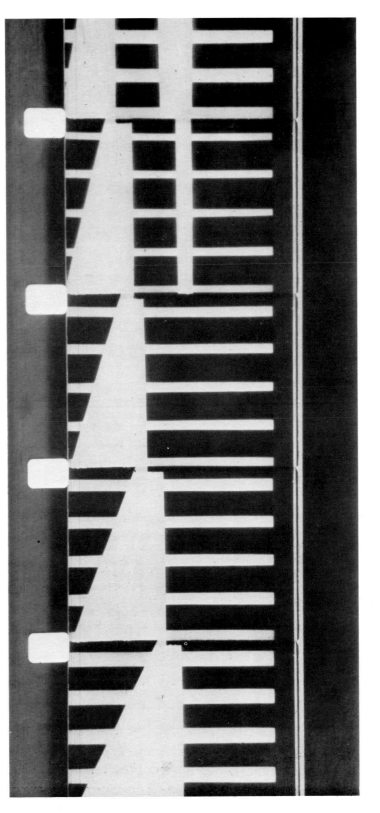

It seems that Ruttmann was trying to move away from the anthropomorphic, symbolic interpretation of his forms, though reluctant to lose the directness of contact this allowed with human experience, not only at the 'dramatic' level, but also at the level of bodily empathy or kinaesthesis. This process is continued in his fourth and final abstract film, *Opus IV*, though some of his later work for Lotte Reiniger's *Prince Achmed* is undeniably abstract. *Opus IV* begins in a most surprising manner, using bold, horizontal stripes moving in relationship to each other. In their strongest form, these are neither symbolist nor geometrically kinetic, but optical, having more in common with the Op Art of the sixties than the geometric abstraction of the twenties (similar in this respect to Duchamp's *Anemic Cinéma*). When the moving horizontal stripes are joined by verticals, the pace becomes frenetic, like riding in a train, but where the speed is experienced through the eyes in relaxed bodily stasis. This sequence prefigures the opening of Ruttmann's *Berlin, Symphony of a City*, where the iron girders of a bridge are seen flashing past from a train window. The final sequences of *Opus IV* return to the geometric kineticism of the third film, but the images seem to be achieved by cut-out templates interacting with each other rather than by the more organic painting technique.

In spite of no clear theory, though Ruttmann and Diebold doubtless talked frequently about the films, they show a significant development, and stand out most clearly in that period as fulfilled works. At the same time, they open up just as many possibilities for the future as do the works of Richter or Eggeling.

Born in 1900, Oskar Fischinger was the youngest of the four Germans active in the early twenties. Like Ruttmann, he was friendly with Diebold, and certainly had been sufficiently interested in the idea of a new, 'abstract' cinema to have collected his various articles. By 1921, Fischinger was clearly already involved in abstract film, if only at the level of intention.[9] He was extremely impressed by the première of Ruttmann's *Opus I* that year, which may have stimulated him to begin practical work, but he is unlikely to have realized anything before late 1922 or early 1923. His family reported that he had no film equipment before he left Frankfurt for Munich in August 1922, though, while unlikely, it is not impossible that he had occasional access to other animation equipment.

Between 1921 and 1923, Fischinger invented an animation system based on successively slicing thin layers from a prepared wax block. The block was prepared in such a way that the movement of the image was contained in the gradual transformation of the object in the depth of the block, rather like the lettering in a stick of seaside rock. He constructed a prototype for Ruttmann who used it for some of the sequences in *Prince Achmed*. Letters show that Fischinger's construction of the machine was almost complete by February 1923, and there survive extensive fragments of film which Fischinger made with it, probably during its development and installation period. There have even been suggestions that Fischinger was a pupil of Ruttmann, as Ruttmann's purchase of the wax-slicing machine did assist Fischinger to get started as a film-maker and kept them in contact for some time. However Moritz says that according to their correspondence Ruttmann did not regard Fischinger as an inferior novice or apprentice, and that they respected the integrity of each other's work and methods as professional rivals.

From 1923, Fischinger began working with an animation company in Munich, making cartoons for commercial release, and about the same time he set up an animation table in his home for his own abstract experiments. Before 1930, and the presentation in some cinemas of his black and white music films, the *Studies*, there is no single abstract film work of the early period which was regularly shown. Nothing from this period survives unequivocally in the form in which it was presented at the time, although Fischinger's archives contain many hundreds of metres of abstract experiments dating from 1923 on, and there is ample evidence that some of these were used in, and possibly were even designed to be used in, multi-projection or a primitive form of 'light-show'. Work by Fischinger was incorporated into the presentations, *Farblichtmusik* (colour-light-music) staged by the composer Alexander Laszlo. Fischinger certainly used sequences of his wax-sliced material in one such presentation in 1926 or 1927, and journalists have reported a three-projector presentation which took place in Fischinger's studio in July 1926 and again in January 1927.

Of the abstract material, fragmentary partly because of deterioration in the nitrate stock, and partly because of the nature of his experiments during that time, some is wax-sliced work known as *Spirals*, some material which pre-figures the linear images of his *Studies*, and, the most impressive, sequences which he called *Orgelstäbe* (literally 'organ-pipes', but translated by Fischinger as *Staffs*). These are a series of explorations on the basic theme of vertical bars of various widths moving up and down in the frame, and may well have formed the basis of his colour experiments using the three-projector superimposition system.

Fischinger's most accessible and important work is that which he did from the thirties on, beginning with the *Studies*. Both during this time, and later in America, he carried the torch for abstract cinema almost alone, making a link with the post-war abstract work there.

Michel. This evening marked the symbolic end of Dada, with Breton reputedly intervening in a performance of Tzara's *Le Coeur à gaz*, wielding his walking-stick and breaking the arm of one performer, Pierre de Massot. The Dadaist intention of Man Ray's film, as well as being responsible for its form, can also hide the significance of the formal consequence of the work. We can be fooled into the assumption that its form is chaotic, because its intention was that it should be. However, like all Dada work it shows that aformalism is an impossibility, for the destruction of one set of formal principles only makes way for the emergence of new ones. The most evident innovation of this film was the application of the techniques of the rayogram to cinematography. Many developments in contemporary avant-garde film were prefigured in some way by the films of this early period. The direct physical action on film embodied in the rayogram principle, foreshadows later developments concerned with the material nature of film.

*Retour à la Raison* is the first film I shall discuss in which the 'abstract' quality is in no way related to the animation of painterly abstract forms. Though Dadaist works did not eschew object reference, as a means of relating their work to the world of 'normal' perception they did not deal in the manipulation of symbolic images or events, which was a Surrealist development. As in other films of the period, because the artists lacked a critical language for the evaluation of their innovations, many of the most interesting notions of this film seem only to have been half-realized and half-seen by Man Ray. They were the result of a scattered intuition in a medium where the plastic possibilities had been almost totally ignored to that date. Such a range of experiment was needed that many of the films pointed in a dozen directions at once.

*Retour à la Raison* brings up at least three possibilities of essentially 'cinematic' abstraction relating to the mechanics, materials, chemistry and techniques of cinematography.

The first is relatively simple and exploited by many film-makers of this time, that is the separation of visual qualities from their object reference. This treats the pattern of light falling on objects and its movement as the basis of experience, deliberately separating it from a specific identification with a particular object. In Man Ray's film, close-up shots of a torso and paper rolls are filmed in such a way as to maintain an ambiguity about their object nature and identity. This form of abstraction usually rests on the use of extreme close-up, extreme lighting, objects in rapid motion, or camera angles which prevent identification or obscure key features of an object.

Second is the synthetic combination through editing of film sequences based on their visual or kinetic relationships, as opposed to the more usual constructing of narrative or symbolic meaning. In this film, images of lights at night in a fairground follow similar points of light on the screen made by the rayogram technique, continuing and orchestrating their visual pattern and motion.

The third possibility is the most complex and most radical, and has no other instance in film (except in Ray's next one) until much later—it is that related to the application of the rayogram technique. Indeed, as the ramifications of this development are complex and central to later themes of this book, I shall only attempt to introduce them at a rudimentary level now. At a number of points in the film, we shift from film shot in

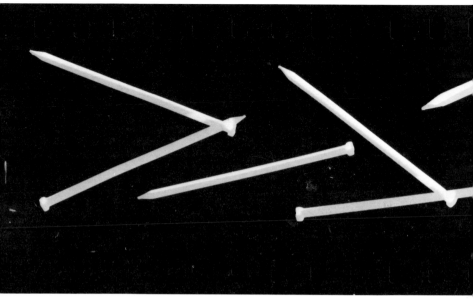

Man Ray: *Retour à la Raison*, 1923 (Enlarged 35mm strip)

the usual way with a camera to images made by laying nails, dust, pins, springs and drawing-pins onto the film and exposing it to light. The image made with this 'rayogram' technique cuts across the separate frame lines, and so, when projected, is often difficult to recognize. The technique serves to provide novel shapes and perception to the film viewer, but it is impossible to separate the effect made from an awareness that these images were the product of a significantly different procedure to that using the camera. Essentially, these sections of Man Ray's film serve to draw attention to the material nature of the film itself and the images on it as a photochemical reality. As an extension of this area of awareness, it becomes impossible to separate the material aspects of the image from the photo-chemical process and the procedural aspects of constructing the work.

To what degree Man Ray 'understood' this development in his own film is difficult to answer. In painting, awareness of the materiality of the object had manifested itself in the application of newspaper to a cubist painting and through the field of collage in general. Rayograms draw attention to this materiality, particularly as in the original photo-graphic plates the actual size of objects is maintained. They also show that Man Ray was concerned to work with techniques which displayed the 'intrinsic' nature of the medium.

Concerning procedure as the basis of content, his friend Duchamp had used documentation of chance procedures as early as 1913 in the work *Three standard stoppages*. We should also remember that Dada was the first movement where activity alone could be considered as art (or anti-art). Man Ray included in his film a sequence of writing scratched 'sideways' along the film 'à tirer 5 fois' (which surely originated as an instruction to print a sequence five times), and in another sequence a line seems to have been made by a lighted match. It would be wrong to see the inclusion of this kind of material, and the film's structure, simply as the result of Dada permissiveness. Man Ray's film must be considered as 'intentional' even if many of its implications were not clear to him. Man Ray considered his second film, *Emak Bakia* (1926), to have been strictly made as a Surrealist work. Certainly it shows a shift away from the material and procedural aesthetic hinted at in his first film, in favour of Surrealist relationships based on symbolic and identity analogies. This tendency progresses in his next two films, *L'Etoile de Mer* (1928) and *Les Mystères du Château de Dé* (1929), which become increasingly narrative in their means. As such I find them both less radical and outside the scope of this book. *Emak Bakia*, however, maintains and develops some of the abstract relationships used in *Retour à la Raison*, and incidentally makes use of a live-action repeat of legs getting out of a car, a filmic notion which had appeared in Léger's *Ballet Mécanique* two years earlier.

Léger's work as a painter needs little introduction. Though broadly attached to the Cubists, his work always contained incongruous, directly drawn figurative elements. His one film, *Ballet Mécanique*, seeks a similar juxtaposition. Some sequences are simply live-action shots, others are animated circles and triangles, and yet others come in-between, either the animation of figurative elements—like disembodied legs from a stocking advertisement—into abstract relationships, or the transformation of normal photography into simple images or shapes. Like Man Ray's first film, there is no single formal direction, but many diverse ideas are tried out. The film is, however, long enough and sufficiently co-ordinated in some formal directions to show that Léger had abandoned any semblance of episodic narrative or symbolic structure in favour of new co-ordinating principles. However many ideas remained undeveloped in *Ballet Mécanique*, Léger was trying to establish a formal unity for the work, fully aware that he sought a film structure based on plastic principles.

Two years after completing the film, Léger wrote an article entitled 'A new realism—the object (its plastic and cinematic graphic value)' in which he says:

Every effort in the line of spectacle or moving picture should be concentrated on bringing out the values of the object—even at the expense of the subject and every other so called photographic element of interpretation, whatever it may be. All current cinema is romantic, literary, historical expressionist, etc. Let us forget all this and consider if you please: a pipe—a chair—a hand—an eye—a typewriter—a hat—a foot, etc., etc.

Let us consider these things for what they can contribute to the screen just as they are—in isolation—their value enhanced by every known means . . .

The technique emphasized is to isolate the object or fragment of an object and to present it on the screen in close-ups of the largest possible scale. Enormous enlargements of an object or a fragment gives it a personality it never had before and in this way it can become a vehicle of entirely new lyric and plastic power . . .

To get the right plastic effect, the usual cinematographic methods

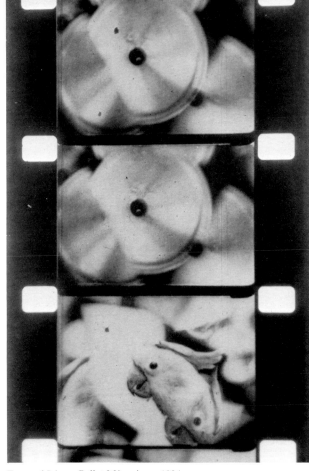

Fernand Léger: Ballet Mécanique, 1924

must be entirely forgotten. The question of light and shade becomes of prime importance. The different degrees of mobility must be regulated by the rhythms controlling the different speeds of projection—'la minuterie'—the timing of projections must be calculated mathematically.[1]

Whatever else this shows, it indicates that Léger had some developed ideas of a general nature about new possibilities for cinematography and how they could be achieved. In particular it shows a grasp of abstract directions for lighting and rhythm. As in the first films of Man Ray, *Ballet Mécanique* makes use of the abstracting techniques which separate the visual qualities of an object from its specific identity. For example, there are a number of sequences in the film of various kitchen implements, chosen for their textural qualities (metallic and partially reflective), and their simple geometric shapes. These qualities are isolated by the framing and the lighting, while the short duration of the sequence frustrates any attempt to identify the object. In the same article Léger says:

Take an aluminium saucepan. Let shafts of light play on it from all angles—penetrating and transforming it. Present it on the screen in a close up, it will interest the public for a time yet to be determined. The public need never know that this fairy-like effect of light in many forms, that so delights it, is nothing but an aluminium saucepan.

Also like Man Ray, Léger develops in his film the idea of linking images on the basis of visual similarity to the extent that the repetition of triangular forms become a major formal basis within the film. As well as the animation of a triangle, intercut with a circle, the triangle reappears continuously in the live-action sequence where mirrors are arranged as a triangular tube in front of the camera lens. This 'kaleidoscope' technique was first introduced into photography by Alvin Langdon Coburn in his vortographs of 1917.

As well as linking sequences through similarities in centrally placed geometric shapes Léger also uses a kinetic linkage based on similarities of movement. Yet in the kinetic linkage, the elements of movement tend to be confined within the screen, like the rotation or pumping action of machine parts, the swinging of a glass ball or a figure on a swing, and never reach the kind of pace which is capable of fully separating experience of movement from other qualities of the object in motion. Rather, movement is orchestrated as a sculptural, rhythmic quality, its direction is used in the shot, and also differentiates qualities such as a gentle oscillation and a mechanical pumping, much in common with Ruttmann's sensibility in his *Opus* series.

It is also the first exploration of another form of rhythm—that constructed from the change of image itself. Lengths of film are used deliberately in a rhythmic beat structure. Though this structure may relate to movement or rhythm within the frame, it is essentially of a more basic order, analogous to the relationship of a drum beat to melody in music. This form of editing was also taken up by Eisenstein, particularly in *October*, by Gance in *Napoleon* and by Vertov in *Man with the Movie Camera*. As with some of the other works of this period, Léger's film was accompanied by a specially composed music score, in this case by George Antheil, which would have considerably heightened the pace and rhythm of the film.

Possibly as a by-product of the rhythmic editing of sequences, Léger, also for the first time in a film, introduces lengths of film with no image —strips of black film—as elements of the rhythmic and optical interchange, and thereby also prefigures a concern within abstract cinema, which later almost takes on the proportions of a 'genre', the flicker effect.

There are two other firsts which can probably be claimed for *Ballet Mécanique*, and which have an important place later. One of these is almost an aside within the film and may have been the result of accident, though some of the implications may well have appealed to Léger when he saw the result. In one sequence a mirrored glass ball is swung backwards and forwards. As well as creating a link with the woman on the swing at the beginning of the film, its circular shape connects it with the circle theme established by the geometric shapes, and its polished surface links it with the dominating metallic quality of many of the objects in the film. But, as the ball swings, the camera and its operator

Fernand Léger: Ballet
Mécanique, 1924

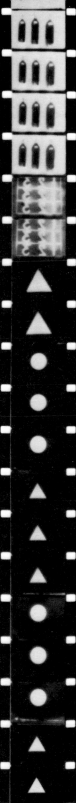

(presumably Dudley Murphy, who is so credited) are mirrored in its surface, creating the first direct reference to the machinery of cinema as part of the content of film. This is a notion which Vertov developed more consistently later, and which anticipates some of the most recent formal notions occupying contemporary film-makers.

The other 'first' is the multiple repetition of a sequence, again prefiguring what is now almost a 'genre'—exploration of the 'loop'. The sequence is of a woman, with a bag on her back, climbing a set of steps, filmed from above. Certainly, the repetition in this sequence is prophetic, for example of Warhol's multiple repeat paintings. But how does it work in Léger's film? It follows a series of sequences of machines which establish certain machine rhythms. In this context the repetition of the woman's movement on the steps could originally have been thought of as the application of machine 'rotation' to the human movement. This is consistent with Léger's paintings, where his figures have the predominant quality of machine parts. It also confirms other statements in his 1926 article, for example referring to a list of objects: 'In this enumeration I have purposedly [sic] included parts of the human body in order to emphasize the fact that in the new realism the human being, the personality, is very interesting only in these fragments and that these fragments should not be considered of any more importance than any of the other objects listed.'

In case the reader is disturbed by the 'inhumanity' of this statement, it should be understood in the context of the period in which it was made. To the Futurist, the development of machinery and manufacture was viewed with optimism as the means by which real human progress might be made. Far from seeming inhuman, the machine was seen as a means of salvation and was celebrated in film by, for example, Vertov, and in a poor copy of aspects of *Ballet Mécanique* by Eugène Deslaw in his *Marche des Machines* (1928). One of the earliest films to consider the effect of the machine on human behaviour in an unfavourable light was *Modern Times* (1936) made by Chaplin, ironically the subject, in cubist form, of the animation sequence which begins and ends *Ballet Mécanique*. The twentieth century and our manner of life, as many of the artists of this period rightly foresaw, has been and will continue to be closely linked to the machine and manufacture. What is important, aesthetically, in the machine references of Léger's film, is the way in which they constitute an appropriate parallel for the mechanical aspect of cinematography itself—a central aspect of the film's meaning.

Another film of this period which broke significantly new ground is more directly abstract in the sense of not including live-action sequences, though very different to the German work. *Anemic Cinéma*, completed in 1926 or 1927, was technically the result of a collaboration between Marcel Duchamp and Man Ray, though there can be no doubt that the film is aesthetically the work of Duchamp. Duchamp himself frequently disclaimed that it was a work of 'cinema', and though his statements are notoriously perverse, there is some significance in this remark, for he had no ambition within this film to engage directly with the problem of the cinematic culture and its language. He wished simply to make use of the techniques which cinematography offered him at that point to solve an artistic problem.

Fernand Léger: Ballet Mécanique, 1924

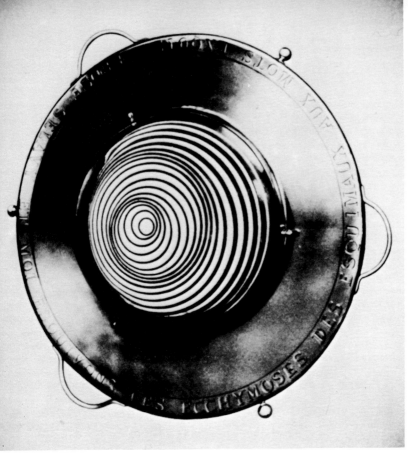

Marcel Duchamp: *Rotary demi-sphere (precision optics)*, 1925.
Optical kinetic device

*right*
Marcel Duchamp: *Anemic Cinéma*, 1926

In its simplest aspect this involved using cinematic projection as a
means of extending his current work on basic optical phenomena. This
had begun with his *Hand stereoscopy* (1918), and continued with the
more directly related *Rotary glass plate (precision optics)* (1920), also
with Man Ray, and with *Rotary demi-sphere (precision optics)* (1925).
This concern with optics had mostly narrowed down to an investigation
of stereoscopic experience, achieved by rotating various configurations of
non-concentric circles. Though often described as 'spirals', none of these
optical discs was strictly a spiral line, the spiral image being a by-product
of the eccentric placing of the circles. Cinematography offered Duchamp
an intense light source and thereby a contrast factor exceeding that of the
printed discs themselves. It also offered a controlled rate of rotation, and
a controlled duration.

In one aspect *Anemic Cinéma* is simply an experiment or demonstration in optics—an examination for the viewer of a particular aspect of
his own optical functioning. However this represented a significant
change in the way in which a work of art functioned for the viewer.

Though abstract work at the time was making use of relationships of geometric forms which were essentially visual, Duchamp's was the first work which attempted to isolate that region of optical experience which is a consequence of our autonomic nervous function. Because this experience is directly dependent on our physiology, some consistency of response could be expected from viewer to viewer. This direction of enquiry could more reasonably hope to discover an area of 'universal' experience (if not language) than was likely in the subjective interpretation of colour and geometric shape in the work of Eggeling or Kandinsky.

*Anemic Cinéma* is not only composed of rotating optical discs, of which there are ten, but each optical unit is separated by a sequence of similarly rotating verbal configurations, this time presented genuinely in spiral form. Any complete grasp of Duchamp's film must include some understanding of these verbal discs. As they are in French, deliberately obscure, this aspect of the work is largely lost on non-French audiences. Valuable work has been done by Katrina Martin,[2] on a form of 'multiplex' interpretive translation, where she examines the phrases, tracing meanings for the words—ambiguities, double-meanings, and puns— and describes some of the structured alliteration at a phonetic level. For example, just as the title is an almost mirror anagram, a fact made evident by the visual style of the titling in the film, Katrina Martin also shows how the last word disc in the film L'ASPIRANT HABITE JAVEL ET MOI J'AVAI L'HABITE EN SPIRALE is more or less a mirror image centring on 'ET MOI'. 'The first syllable corresponds to the last, and so on: L'AS : ALE/ SPIR : SPIR/ ANT : EN/ HABITE : HABITE/ JAVEL : J'AVAIS L'.'

For the most part, all the verbal discs are susceptible to some structural analysis of this kind. Further, it is within the overall conception of the film that such semantic structures should be interspersed with the optical discs. Martin has also pointed out that the spatial experience of being drawn into or thrown out from the centres of the optical discs is altered and made 'interpretive' by juxtaposition with the frequently sexual connotations of the verbal discs. In addition the length of time the spectator is given to absorb the verbal material conditions the extent of semantic speculation which can be undertaken as the film is seen. All in all, the film has complex ramifications, as does all Duchamp's work, further complicated by his intentional system of autobiographical, symbolic cross-reference.

Whether or not Duchamp intended it, his film does contribute a significant innovation in cinema, and like all the other films so far discussed represents the first indication of concerns which form the basis of more consistent development in work of a later period.

Considering the difficulties, films produced in France and Germany represent a surprisingly radical range of formal possibilities. Though contemporary work in avant-garde cinema has now clarified and extended the directions opened up in that period, the consequences have still not been felt in our popular film culture.

# 4 · Premature decline

Excepting the very early Italian experiments of Ginna and Corra, the most exciting period of innovation is contained in the five years from 1921 to 1926. Talking of the 1925 show of international avant-garde films in Berlin, Hans Richter later said: 'If we felt before this international avant-garde film show more or less as an "avant" without a "garde" at the back of us, we did not feel so any more after it. The existence of *Entr'acte* and *Ballet Mécanique* (maybe there were more films, but I don't remember them any more) proved that we belonged to something.'[1]

Yet however much Richter and others began to sense that they 'belonged to something', it could not be said that there had been a real movement. During the five years from 1921, there were little more than a dozen genuinely independent works produced, by at best eight or nine artists. There was a considerable geographical separation between the artists, and the opportunities for seeing the films under good conditions were few and far between, especially where live music was incorporated in the presentation. Compare this to the situation in any other field of art, where a continuous flow of works by a large number of artists, regularly exhibited, creates a real cultural impetus and interchange of ideas. New directions are worked out, presented, criticized and new positions developed quickly. Perhaps most important, this flow of ideas keeps 'in step' with contemporary developments in other fields, such interchange being essential if a medium is to develop as an art form of contemporary relevance. Experiment with film as a plastic art form at that time did not develop that kind of impetus. Considering the financial, cultural and technical difficulties which the film-makers faced, surprising and exceptional innovations were made, but even so, we should only consider the work of that time as a primitive beginning. From 1926 until just before the 1939 war, the pace of development slowed down, and with some notable exceptions, no new ground was covered. If anything, it became even less of a 'movement'.

Ruttmann's success drew him increasingly into collaboration on commercial ventures, until he finally became submerged as a talented editor within the film industry of the Third Reich. Richter also produced some commercial work, but even his self-financed experimental films, with one exception, did not consolidate or extend the most radical aspects of his earlier work. Man Ray's Surrealist tendency was a somewhat retrogressive return to the narrative forms of conventional cinema. Eggeling died in 1925; Duchamp was never concerned with cinema as such; Léger found the production problems too time-consuming to make another film, though he did design the sets for Alexander Korda's *Things to Come* in 1934, as he had already done with Marcel L'Herbier's *L'Inhumaine* (1923).

Though Fischinger did most significant work this period is essentially one of decline in experiment. There are also important individual works by Richter, Ruttmann, Vertov and Moholy-Nagy, and a broad new tendency—a new form of documentary concept—which has some

his own name removed from the credits. Paul Rotha also points out that the presentation of *Potemkin* in Berlin in 1926 had also contributed to Ruttmann's subsequent editing of Freund's material.

However, the film still has many interesting qualities and formal concepts. Its documentary form is the first example of a 'cross-sectional' structure. Though there are certain linear developments along various themes, the general structure is a cross-section impression of the texture of a city's life. This gives reign to Ruttmann's major talent, the connection of images on the basis of their abstract visual and kinetic qualities. This is seen particularly in the opening sequence shot from a train. For some time, the screen is dominated by images of girders and railway tracks which smear past at great pace, separating themselves almost completely from their object origins. Combined with the strobe effect caused by the camera shutter, this creates a highly 'cinematic' abstraction, a fusion of the inherent function of the camera, the velocity of the motion and the play of light and dark.

*Berlin* and the other work of this period continually pose political questions. The most fundamental of these is how radicalism in the formal aspect of cinema can be related to radical politics, particularly raised by the work of Dziga Vertov. But first there is the more obvious problem of finance. Film has never been a cheap medium to use: the machinery, the raw materials and the chemical processing are all costly. During the twenties, all the films were made on expensive 35mm, which remains the most common gauge for the commercial cinema; 16mm was introduced in the USA as an amateur medium (the original home-movie gauge) in 1923, but its spread was slow, coming too late for the European experimenters to consider its use as an alternative to 35mm. In fact, the post-war expansion of the much cheaper 16mm facilities, and its use by experimental film-makers, is probably the single most important factor in the emergence of a real alternative film culture.

By the twenties the large production companies and corporations had a stranglehold on the lucrative mass entertainment medium of film. Artists like Eggeling, Richter and Fischinger set up improvised animation equipment in their own studios in an attempt to give themselves uninterrupted conditions of work. But this did not free them from financial restraints, and dealing with the resulting technical problems contributed to the slow pace of development. The energy needed to maintain an independent approach to film was enormous: the artists were both struggling with a technically difficult medium and having to raise money for an approach to film which showed little hope of a quick financial return.

As a result, Man Ray found a rich backer (*Les Mystères du Château du Dé*, his last film, was financed by the Comte de Noailles, as was Buñuel and Dali's *L'Age d'Or*); Richter and Fischinger subsidized independent films by commercial work; Ruttmann tried to work directly through the industry. An alternative, visualized by Moholy-Nagy, was a form of public subsidy, or the establishment of institutions for film experiment, which, in recent years, has begun to materialize to some extent through public grants and film studies within art institutions. In his case the Bauhaus formed the background for his own experimentation, but film was never really established there.

If artists had found it difficult to get access to film facilities and finance before 1927 and maintain a complete independence to pursue their aesthetic impulses, after 1927, and Jolson's *The Jazz Singer*, when the whole industry went over to the 'talkie', it became almost impossible. When the cinema relied wholly on its images, the image-makers were held in some esteem, but the introduction of sound only consolidated the dominance of theatre and literature. By the end of the thirties, the cinema was established as a major profitable industry, quite clearly a major capitalist enterprise.

The exception to this is Revolutionary Russia, which leads to Dziga Vertov.

# 5 · 'Filmdrama is the opium of the masses'

Many of the artists seeking a new formal basis for cinema expressed a direct opposition to its theatrical and narrative background, but no film-maker of the period understood this problem as clearly as the Russian Dziga Vertov, and few since have expressed this opposition with his fervour and flair. Vertov was no academic theoretician, but in a polemical manner aimed to eliminate the gap between theory and practice. He always demanded to be able to think through the practice of film-making. Before the October Revolution he had studied at the Moscow Psycho-Neurological Institute, a point which has some significance in his statements and later editing style.

Born in 1896, Vertov came of age at the outbreak of the Revolution. In Moscow, Mayakovsky, as a Futurist poet, could hardly be avoided, and Vertov, who also for a time wanted to be a poet, adopted much of Mayakovsky's aggressive public style and terse writing. It was Alexandre Lemberg, the son of a cameraman, who introduced Vertov to cinema and his first practical experiments. Within seven months of the Bolshevik revolution, he was, as secretary of the Skobelev committee (the newly formed state film production unit), in at the very beginning of Soviet film production with the release of the first cinema weekly. With a team which included cameramen Giber, Tisse and Ermlov, and the editor Elizabeta Svilova (his future wife), by the summer of 1918 he had become the centre of the operation.

There can be no doubt that Lenin saw this work as being of fundamental importance: in a period when all accounts are of shortage of film-stock and equipment, by 1919, Vertov had not only produced nearly fifty of the weekly newsreels, but also three general compilation films. Before beginning his next major set of newsreels, *Kinopravda* ('film truth'), in 1922 he had produced a number of other films. He had been a major figure in establishing and running a film-car on the agit-train of President Kalinin in 1920, which had facilities for shooting, developing, editing and projecting film daily throughout their travels in the Russian provinces.

In Russia, as elsewhere, the dominant mode of cinema was the film-drama, having its roots deeply in the forms of literature and theatre. In its earliest days, cinema had been popular in a way very similar to music hall or vaudeville, and the earliest short films were often produced by people who had worked in that situation. At a primitive level they were simple entertainment 'sketches' of a vaudeville kind. Not only was their main audience the urban working-class, but for some time their production roots were largely from the same section of society. The rise of the more sophisticated, longer narrative film occurred simultaneously with the invasion of business interests into cinema. In a gradual process cinema established a particular social function and with it forms which engendered a particular kind of psychological reaction from its audience. Though the roots of its content remained in the fantasies and aspirations of the working-class, the manipulation and resolution of these fantasies through film came increasingly under the control of the films' financiers.

They encouraged films that conditioned the fantasies of the mass audience in ways which would create no threat to the current social order—a function taken over now by television. It can be argued that any society involves repression, particularly of sexual and aggressive behaviour. The commercial cinema, having taken as its basis of content the fantasies, fears, aspirations and tensions of society, forms around them cinematic conventions intended to create a popular acceptance of the existing social order. Other commentators begin to see this at the relatively simple level of plot, the dramatic resolution of the various subjects in film. There is another level to this issue: not only should we look at the reactionary nature of a film's 'message'—the social meaning implicit in the resolution of its plot—but we should also be concerned with the manner of perception and response which is engendered in the formal construction of a work.

In many respects, the formal construction of illusionist cinema has a more basic effect than the stories themselves. A 'revolutionary' story, which creates an essentially passive response in the audience, may be as reactionary in its social effect as a story which has no revolutionary aspirations. In theatre, this is a problem which Bertolt Brecht was the first to express clearly. In cinema, awareness of the political implications of form is first clearly expressed in the writings of Vertov and the Kino-Eye group. In 1920 Vertov wrote:

1 Filmdrama is the opium of the masses.
2 Down with the immortal kings and queens of the screen! Long live the ordinary people filmed in every day life and at work!
3 Down with the bourgeois imagination and its fairytales! Long live everyday life!
4 Filmdrama and religion are deadly weapons in the hands of the capitalists. Only through showing our revolutionary daily life do we strike the weapon from the enemy's hand.
5 The modern art-drama is a relic of the old world. It is an attempt to press our revolutionary reality into reactionary forms![1]

In 1924, he shows his awareness of the reactionary effect of conventional narrative cinema and thus the link between politics and the mode of perception engendered in the film audience:

If we want to understand clearly the effect of films on the audience, we have first to agree about two things:
1 What audience?
2 What effect upon the audience are we talking about?
On the movie-house habitué, the ordinary fiction film acts like a cigar or cigarette on a smoker. Intoxicated by the cine-nicotine, the spectator sucks from the screen the substance which soothes his nerves.[2]

And later from the same discussion:

To intoxicate and suggest—the essential method of the fiction film approximates it to a religious influence, and makes it possible after a certain time to keep a man in a permanent state of overexcited unconsciousness . . . Musical shows, theatrical and cine-theatrical performances and so on above all act upon the subconscious of the spectator or listener, distorting his protesting consciousness in every possible way.

Dziga Vertov: *Man with the Movie Camera*, 1929

**Consciousness or Subconsciousness**

We rise against the collusion between the 'director-enchanter' and
the public which is submitted to the enchantment.

The conscious alone can fight against magical suggestions of every
kind.

The conscious alone can form a man of firm convictions and
opinions.

We need a conscious people, not an unconscious mass ready to
yield to any suggestion.

There can be little doubt about the vehemence with which Vertov and
his famous Kino-Eye group viewed the function of the prevalent culture
of cinema and its forms. He was certain that the history of cinema to

that date had succumbed to a pervasive reactionary content, and he was also aware that this deeply infected the language, convention and forms of cinema and the habitual responses of its audience. He knew that his task was a practical one—to establish a strong new form—and this meant experiment with the means and functions of cinema. It implied a radical rethinking of all assumptions, an attitude in common with the experimenters active in France, Germany and Italy, but of whom Vertov would have had little knowledge at this time.

Although at the beginning Vertov settled on the alternative of newsreel or documentary, his own development leading to *Man with the Movie Camera* (1929), and a close look at other statements he made, indicate that his approach was not simply one of the 'actuality film' against fictional cinema. The strength of his polemical statements should not be seen to imply a rigid dogmatism in their practical application, since experiment was essential to discovery of new forms. Between 1922 and 1925, whilst he had control over *Kinopravda*, he also organized the other major newsreel enterprise *Goskinokalendar*, and used *Kinopravda* increasingly for the experimentation of the Kino-Eye group.

Dziga Vertov: *Man with the Movie Camera*, 1929

As he was violently opposed to the scenario as the basis of film and deeply committed to catching life 'unawares', it is not surprising that his main attention focussed on the shooting and editing stages. Kino-Eye had never considered the camera as a substitute for the human eye, but had always affirmed it as a machine in its own terms capable of extending or creating new perception. Vertov stated: ' "Kino-Eye" makes use of all the new techniques for high speed representation of movement, micro-cinematography, reversed movement, multiple exposures etc.'; and: ' "Kino-Eye" does not regard these as mere tricks or special effects but as a normal technique which should be used as widely as possible.'[3]

Before considering how Vertov's concept of editing constitutes his major formal contribution to film, I would like to illustrate a little further the link Vertov's experimentation in this period has with that of his European contemporaries. He reports the invention of new film genres by the *Kinopravda* group as follows: 'Review films, sketch films, verse films, film poems and preview films made their appearance . . . Considerable work was done in the utilization of new methods for subtitling, transforming titles into pictorial units equal to the images.'[4] The inclusion in this list of 'verse films' and 'film poems', together with his expressed annoyance after seeing René Clair's *Paris qui dort* (1926) that Kino-Eye had not made such a film first, suggests strongly to me that he would have also been greatly impressed by all the work already described, particularly Léger's *Ballet Mécanique*.

It is interesting to note that Léger, far from seeing his own 'abstraction' as being in conflict with realism, considered it to be the 'new realism'. In fact, work which affirms the basic material and processes of its own medium has more claim to the term 'realist' than that which denies the medium in favour of simulating life, which deserves the title 'illusionist'. (In many respects this represents a reversal of popular usage.) Vertov's development of a greater fragmentation in temporal continuity certainly did not, for him, contradict the 'realist' nature of his work:

'Kino-Eye' employs all the resources of montage describing simultaneously phenomena from opposite poles of the universe, in an order which may be chronological or not at will, violating, if necessary, the conventions and precedents for the construction of a 'kino-object'.

'Kino-Eye', flinging itself into the heart of the apparent disorder of life, strives to find in life itself the answers to the questions it asks: to find amongst a mass of possibilities the correct, the necessary fact to solve the theme.

'Kino-Eye' is:

montage—when I set myself a theme (one chosen from thousands)
montage—when I take care to guard against irrelevancies in developing the theme (to make the only appropriate choice from thousands of observations)
montage—when I decide upon the order in which the filmed material will be presented (to choose from amongst thousands of possible combinations the one that seems most appropriate, bearing in mind the nature of the filmed material itself or the demands of the chosen theme).[5]

In case Vertov gives the impression that he was only concerned with relationships in the symbolic and semantic sense, and that his idea of theme was literary, the continuation of the quotation shows that there was no such convenient separation of the semantic from the material aspects of his film images.

The 'Kino-Eye' school demands that the construction of the film should be based on the 'intervals' of movement between different planes, on the correct relationship of these intervals to each other and on the movement of one visual impression to another . . . To find the best route for the eye of the spectator to penetrate the chaos of the mutual reactions, attractions, repulsions of images on each other: to reduce these innumerable 'intervals' (intervals of movement between one image and another) to one simple equation, to one spectacular formula which presents, in the best possible way, the essential theme of the film. These are tasks which the director must fulfil.

From an understanding of Vertov's process in constructing a film-reality—a 'film-understanding' out of direct articulation of the material—it is possible to see the essential difference between his concept of montage and the other dominant school of Russian montage, that stemming principally from Eisenstein. Although the notion of 'collision' and its parallel in 'dialectical' thought, articulated by Eisenstein, contribute to Vertov's sensibility, and both share a dynamic sense of motion within editing, Eisenstein's essential purpose remained that of using cinema to create an expressive narrative. In this respect, his innovations in editing were only a means towards this end. Viewed in this way, Eisenstein breaks much less with conventional cinema than does Vertov. For Vertov, editing was essentially a process, and as such a way of structuring the raw materials of film-thought—the collected 'shots'—and thereby structuring experience. The active process of thinking-through-editing is the central process of his film, and, fortunately for us, this did not remain a theoretical idea, but was realized in *Man with the Movie Camera*.

This massive work, whose emergent theme is the inter-relatedness of activity, enterprise and movement of the Soviet metropolis, functions through the most intricate weave of thematic connections. The basis of these connections is multi-levelled, but clear. For example, the sequences interplay at the level of surface distribution of light and dark patterning; they interplay at the levels of direction and rate of movement; they establish, in relationship to these other factors, the independent rhythmic beat of the intercutting rate. But in addition to this co-ordination at the visual and kinetic level, thematic relationships are continually established through identification of the material. These themes are maintained in a developing flux, for as well as the general theme, based on the pattern of activity as it increases and subsides throughout a day in the metropolis, other sub-theme relationships are being woven: comparisons of bodily movement in work and recreation, bodily movements with machine movements, machines with radio communication, music and speech with the gramophone, and so on. In order to create this weave, a temporal simultaneity is effected by clusters of short sequences of images intercut in rapid succession. Though a precision in these relationships is sought and achieved in the film's editing, the spectator

Dziga Vertov: *Man with the Movie Camera*, 1929
*right*
Dziga Vertov: *Man with the Movie Camera*, 1929

always participates in synthesizing the material for himself. One of the film's many significant aspects is the change in behaviour which is elicited from the spectator. It clearly makes impossible the passive, cathartic, emotionally manipulated mode which is normal in the popular cinema culture. This is achieved by the manner and process of the film's editing, and is further reinforced by the direct reference to the machinery.

This is the first film which clearly defines the camera as a participant in what it sees, and is a forerunner of several recent films which explore self-referential structures. It contains film of the camera itself, of projection machines, the cinema auditorium and public, the cinema screen, the film within the film, and the selection of shots at the editing table. In addition, the film explores various forms of superimposition and split-screen forms, which further assist the complex networks of connections. He frequently uses this to establish idea relationships, as in the super-imposition of a singer within a gramophone loudspeaker, but also for various kinds of counter-motion, as in the three-way horizontal division of the screen with tram-cars moving in alternating directions.

Eisenstein's film with most in common in its montage conception is *October*, completed nine months earlier. Whilst I consider this to be the best example of Eisenstein's editing, and the work most structured towards an active perceptual mode in the spectator, even here, he did not really escape a form which was basically manipulative of the audience. In fact, as conditions changed in Russia and the kind of film which was called for was one which could re-inforce nationalistic tendencies, Eisenstein's work regressed into a form which was basically little different to that of the capitalist cinema. It was increasingly used to tell

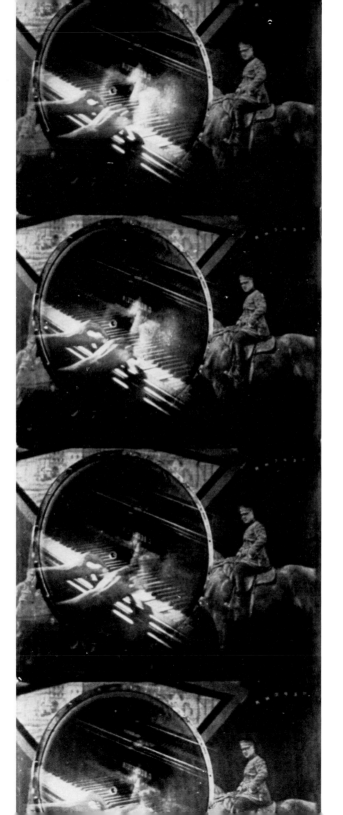

fantasy tales which did nothing to arouse or maintain a revolutionary consciousness in its Russian audience.

Vertov, subsequently accused of being a formalist as Stalinist nationalism gained strength, was never able to develop his fundamental principles further. With the decline of Eisenstein, *Man with the Movie Camera* is the high point of Soviet cinema. Together with Vertov's theoretical statements, it creates the basis for considering how formal innovation in film and radical politics can be related.

Dziga Vertov: *Man with the Movie Camera*, 1929

# 6 · Link

The most innovative work by the early experimental film-makers was done before 1930. As much of the experimental energy had come from Europe, particularly Germany, the rise of Hitler made conditions for radical art in general, and film in particular, extremely difficult. Formal artists, including Richter, were considered decadent and dangerous sources of independent thought. In addition, the economic slump provided a lean time for the consolidation of a film culture based on new formal principles. There is, however, one major exception, Oskar Fischinger, who, having begun to make some contribution in the late twenties, carried on a consistent thread of abstract experiment through the thirties. He also provides an important link with the movement which grew up after the war in America. In addition to Fischinger, the other figure to make a significant contribution in the thirties is Len Lye, working in Britain, who has also spent most of his time in the USA since the war.

I have considered Oskar Fischinger's career up to about 1927. In the summer of that year, for financial reasons, he left Munich for Berlin, foreseeing better prospects for himself at the centre of the German film industry. Fischinger chose to walk the three hundred miles to Berlin, fortunately taking his camera with him and shooting a time-lapse document of the journey. There is no record of his ever having considered this a film for public screening, but an excellent copy survives, has been transferred to 16mm from the original 35mm and now is presented under the label on Fischinger's can: *München-Berlin-Wanderung*. Though the film is made with the attitude of a casual, personal diary, in recent years some film-makers have taken up the time-lapse technique as a serious formal base.

By July of 1928, Fischinger had landed himself a contract in Berlin as a special effects animator at the UFA studios, initially to work on Fritz Lang's science-fiction film *Frau im Mond*. The film, containing Fischinger's contribution, was released in the summer of 1929, but the Nazis later destroyed all known copies, apparently because of the accuracy of the rocketry information. He terminated his UFA contract in 1929 and in the next three years enjoyed considerable success with his own work, for though he continued to take on commercial contracts in the form of advertisements and special effects animation, his independent abstract films began to appear and be shown with increasing interest.

By 1933 Fischinger had completed up to fourteen of his *Studies* series, and made at least two other abstract films in addition to his commercial work, while still finding time to experiment with a form of synthetic optical soundtrack. From 1930 on sound became increasingly important to him, and his attempt to produce a direct form of synthetic optical soundtrack was neither the first (that honour probably belongs to work, in 1929, of the Swiss animator Rudolf Pfenninger), nor would it be the last.

In abstract animation, innovation in form is often linked to innovation in technique. In the history of the whole field of new film-form,

latter idea was, incidentally, welcome, as it allowed reprinting of a sequence, not only lengthening the film with no extra work, but also allowing a second or third look at a complex sequence—a device as valuable as reprise in music. The films, even when viewed 'silent' have a clear musical structure: interweaving linear forms, explosions and climaxes, repeats, partial repeats and variations. The films of this time, all the so-called *Studies*, are best generalized as being a form of abstract choreography, the dance of abstract elements. This leads us to the other major aesthetic problem of this period of Fischinger's work, that of anthropomorphic interpretation.

In the same way that there is an ambivalence in his attitude to music, there is also an ambivalence in his attitude to representational figuration. Much of his early commercial work was in figurative animation, but there also exist a number of examples of independent experiments right up to 1927, in particular a group of experiments under the title *Seelische Konstruktionen* ('spiritual constructions'). These include some fine sequences using wax puppets—in a fight between two boxers their shapes are transformed by the blows which they deal out to each other—and also a figurative use of the wax-slicing machine based on drunken transformations of objects into extreme grotesques. The dramatic, anthropomorphic interpretation of his shapes and their style of movement is a dominant factor in all the 'charcoal-drawn' films. Like the first two or three of Ruttmann's films, to which Fischinger's work during this period owes some allegiance (though certainly not plagiarism), all the studies allow some degree of anthropomorphic interpretation, encouraged by their synchronization to music.

The formal development which is evident through the whole of Oskar Fischinger's work is similar to the changes of emphasis and direction which took place in a compressed way in Ruttmann's series *Opus I* to *IV*. Of course, Fischinger developed every stage with much greater complexity, and any parallel between the two artists must be drawn carefully. Ruttmann touched on many possibilities in a brief flare of activity. Fischinger explored deeply wherever his aesthetic led him so that his work became a complex container for his emotional experience. The path from anthropomorphic forms and movement through geometric relationships to optical interactions could be viewed as a kind of inevitable and logical sequence in the evolution of abstract art in general. The early landscape abstraction of Kandinsky leads to the Constructivist's use of geometric forms, and ends up as the forerunner of Op Art in paintings like Mondrian's *Broadway Boogie-Woogie*.

Fischinger's second period, the geometric, begins with *Kreise* ('circles') made in 1933. His first film in colour, it was also the first ever to use the new, three-colour separation technique, Gasparcolour (which his work on this film helped to perfect). Although it was made as an advertising film, Fischinger ensured that the rights returned to him after six months, and designed it in such a way that the company name could both be replaced by any other company who wanted to buy a version (which they did), and eliminated altogether in his own release of 1934. It is a highly dynamic film which exploits the bold geometric coloured circles, and particularly exploited the new colour process in a way which no commercial user ever did, and only to be matched by Len Lye a couple of years later.

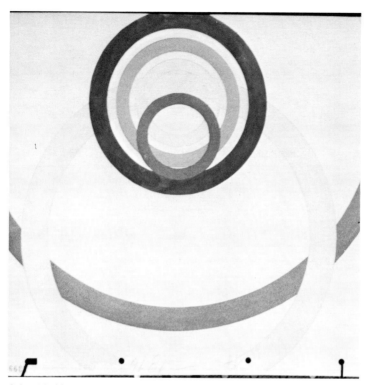

Oskar Fischinger: *Kreise*, 1933. Animation drawing for the film

His earlier geometric experiments, the *Orgelstäbe* (possibly of 1925), were probably projected in a superimposed form with coloured filters. It could be that Fischinger awaited the advent of colour before he took up the problem of bold geometric areas, and he was certainly not satisfied with a version of the linear charcoal films which he coloured afterwards. *Kreise* was closely followed by *Quadrate* ('squares') which he never released, though there is a surviving copy which shows continued experiment with Gasparcolour. Much of the remaining work which he did in Germany, before leaving for America in 1935, fits his exploration of geometric form in colour, including his well-known cigarette advertisements for Muratti and his last film completed in Germany, the *Komposition in Blau* ('composition in blue') of 1935. Like the Muratti films, this film is produced by a pixillation, rather than an animation technique: a frame-by-frame movement of three-dimensional models—cubes and columns. About the same time Fischinger also shot and edited a film document of a walking trip in Switzerland.[1]

The remainder of Fischinger's work was done in the USA, following the offer of a contract from Paramount in 1936. *Komposition in Blau* had just won the Grand Prix in Venice and, together with *Study 8*, a special prize in Belgium, all of which served to draw attention from the Nazi government to his 'decadent' abstraction.

Fischinger had a difficult time in Hollywood, and in general produced

67

his independent work there much more slowly than he had begun to do in Europe. But even if he produced less work, he did not stagnate, continuing to develop his aesthetic into a new phase. The large studios cared less about the work of an experimental film-maker than they did about making sure no one else exploited him whilst they did not. While Fischinger kept trying to work as part of the commercial cinema, his salvation as a film-maker came through the channels of the art-world, in the form of seven years of assistance from the Guggenheim Foundation. His main impact as a film-maker came in his influence on an emerging American movement which gradually became more and more separate from the film industry, establishing an alternative exhibition and distribution system. Fischinger's American films, including *Allegretto* (1936) and *An Optical Poem* (1937), all released after 1940, belong with the beginning of the American abstract film movement.

Fischinger's late period, which saw a new formal development to his work, seemed to reflect the pace and energy of his new environment in much the same way as the late Mondrian paintings did. In fact there is more than a slight similarity in the feeling and style of Mondrian's New York 'optical' paintings and Fischinger's first American film *Allegretto*. Many of the same qualities exist in the similar but more perfect *Radio Dynamics* (1941) which, in spite of its title, was deliberately made without music. Not only is the film free of any representational interpretation because of the lack of music, but the forms themselves create a strong, internal development and motion. The capability of a work to establish its own material and perceptual logic is the intrinsic aim of 'concrete' art, and Fischinger's American work, with the exception of certain aspects of *An American March*, represents a high point in this aim not just in film but within art in general.

At this period, Fischinger was taking the opportunity offered by the commercial studios to work with the technique of transparent cell animation. Unrestrained by any of the conventions which had become attached to the method, his work began to explore new fields of multi-layered form. *An American March* is the least 'pure' film of this period, most affected by the slickness of the Disney style, which he encountered when he worked, without result, on *Fantasia*. Even so, the film is extraordinarily prophetic of the brash qualities and icons which painters of the Pop Art movement, like Roy Lichtenstein and Robert Indiana, later found so engaging. After 1942, until his death in 1967, Fischinger completed fewer and fewer independent films, needing the income from small commercial contracts to survive. He turned increasingly to painting, and his last important complete film is based on the gradual transformations of a 'painting', *Motion Painting No. 1* (1947). This was not a documentary, but a painting done on perspex and filmed frame-by-frame as the images developed. Compared with the dynamism of all his other work, this is a very static concept of animation, but as a result of his awareness of the technique's limitation, Fischinger produced an unexpectedly fine film.

Among other experiments of this time, he returned to the synthetic sound problem, took up problems of stereoscopy, leaving a fragment of this work ready to be printed, and in 1950, with the invention of his Lumigraph, joined the list of people who have produced light organs and light machines.

Oskar Fischinger: *Allegretto*, 1936

Oskar Fischinger: *Radio Dynamics*, 1941

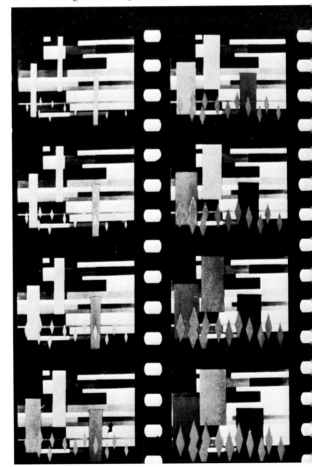

Before moving on to the post-war developments in America which Fischinger helped to initiate, I would like to return to the European scene and particularly to the work of Len Lye. The conditions under which Lye made his most important contribution in Britain were somewhat special. Though he would probably have produced important films in any case, the specific direction he took depended on a set of circumstances engineered by John Grierson through the Empire Marketing Board, and after 1933 the General Post Office. Like Dziga Vertov, Grierson was in almost complete opposition to the fictional film, and, though essentially concerned with documentary cinema, by his support of Len Lye and Norman McLaren, showed that he also endorsed the value of formal experiment.

Len Lye was born in New Zealand in 1901, and studied animation in Australia, where he is reported to have made his first hand-drawn film as early as 1921. Arriving in England in 1927, he quickly sought out what he could of avant-garde cinema through the London Film Society, whose members financially assisted the completion of Len Lye's first film in Britain, *Tusalava*. Finished in 1929, based entirely on animation of 'aboriginal' shapes, it displayed Lye's abstract tendencies. Also through the Film Society, in 1929 Lye worked with Hans Richter on a film in which Eisenstein played a London policeman, both Richter and Eisenstein having been invited to the workshop at the society by its director Ivor Montague. Richter's film titled *Everyday* was finally completed and released in 1968. As a result of the difficulties of making *Tusalava*, Lye could not face another film project for some five years.

His next work began from a point which was extreme in economy and as technically direct as he could imagine—drawing straight onto the celluloid. In this case, again assisted by the film-makers in the Film Society, he used clear film on which an optical soundtrack had already been printed, and to which he could synchronize his drawn images. It is doubtful if Lye knew of the Corra brothers' innovation in this field, but even in Britain he was not alone in developing this direction. Norman McLaren at Glasgow School of Art had made hand-drawn non-abstract film as early as 1933. It would be difficult to unravel the influence the two men had on each other, since by 1936 they were in close contact through their work at the GPO. It is however unfortunate that the subsequent work of McLaren is much better known than that of Lye. In fact, Lye's films are almost impossible to see in Britain, whereas Norman McLaren's adoption and promotion by the Canadian Film Board has resulted in the popular assumption that experimental and abstract film is 'Norman McLaren'. Whilst he has produced a number of pleasant and interesting works, he has only a minor place in the development of new film form. Unlike Lye, he has never been a major formal innovator. Lye's claims as an innovator do not rest simply on his use of hand-painting on clear celluloid but on what he achieved with the technique. Also his most important contribution is perhaps in another aspect of his experimentation, the development of film-printing techniques to exploit the new possibilities in colour film.

Having begun his hand-drawn film experiments in 1935, Lye showed the results to Grierson with a proposal that they should form the basis of a GPO promotion film. To his surprise this was accepted, and the abstract *Colour Box* was widely released in that year, making a considerable impact on film-makers. Subsequently, the hand-drawn film has become something of a genre itself, particularly through the work of Norman McLaren and Lye's late films when he returned to the technique after 1953. Though as a genre it is important, the concept of working directly onto film by hand contributes to another, more fundamental direction, that began with Man Ray's *Retour à la Raison*. Len Lye's attitude to this method has helped to develop an awareness of the material aspects of film as a major basis of language and content. In addition, these material qualities also tend to become an integral part of the images produced. Almost as a by-product, many of the material aspects of film's projection, like the screen, the light projected on it and the directional motion of the film through the projector, all become apparent as a consequence of the hand-drawn technique. Factors which would be seen as 'errors' in conventional animation, like slight off-registration of the successive images, are almost unavoidable in the hand-drawn film, and actually contribute to the material awareness. Slight jitter, and random shifts in the image, serve to show and express the nature of film as a succession of single frames.

Lye in particular seems to have been aware of and welcomed these material qualities, working with, rather than against the 'imperfections'. Many of the marks in *Colour Box* are made by scratching, others by bold stencils repeated from frame to frame with changes of position and colour. This early work forms the basis of his sympathy for the film material which led to his most beautiful calligraphic film, the black-and-white *Free Radicals* (1957) made in the USA, and also to the boldness of his experiments with Gasparcolour, best seen in *Rainbow Dance* (1936) and *Trade Tattoo* (1937).

Because these last two films prefigure, in an extraordinarily versatile and accomplished way, another major direction of the later movement, that based on the transformation of film images through printing and developing techniques, it is worth considering their technical and aesthetic achievement quite closely. Gasparcolour, like the Technicolour system which followed it, is based on the separate application of the three, light-primary dyes, cyan, magenta, and yellow from which all colours can be obtained by mixing. The synthesis of 'natural' colour was achieved by a camera which recorded a prismatically split image on three rolls of monochrome film. Len Lye, like Oskar Fischinger, had different ideas about it. They saw at once that the synthetic process need not be used simply to reconstruct a previous colour analysis, but could form the basis of any kind of colour manipulation. Lye realized that live-action sequences could be transformed both in colour and in their relationship to their backgrounds so that they could be treated as graphic elements, equivalent to non-representational, abstract shapes.

*Rainbow Dance* is deliberately boisterous and amusing. The images bounce along in a cascade of abstract stripes and cross-hatched strokes, filling in the background to 'live' film of a walker with an umbrella who becomes a tennis player. For most of the film this figure is a silhouette, whose colour changes frequently against a drawn or animated background. At one point he executes a tennis stroke, jumping across the screen leaving a series of successive images in different colours behind him—a precursor of McLaren's influential *Pas de deux* (1968). Yet for all the exuberance of the film, it is the result of a carefully planned and

executed 'travelling-matte' technique. This is achieved through a series of negative and positive printings which by masking allow the separation of a figure from its surroundings so that a new background can be added, or the figure given a new colour or texture.

In his next film, *Trade Tattoo*, all the flamboyant technique of *Rainbow Dance* is brought to a fine synthesis, not only between Lye's various technical directions—the hand-painted images and textures, the strong added colour, the intricate travelling-mattes, the use of negative images—but also between the live-action images, which are of a more

Len Lye: *Rainbow Dance*, 1936

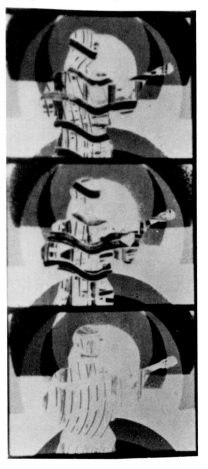

serious nature, and the abstract features. As the film's 'subject' is the importance of postal communications in industry, Lye made use of filmed sequences of industry, possibly even taken from the discarded material of the documentary film-makers with whom he worked at the GPO. This film shows an ability to handle montage which Vertov himself would have appreciated. Amongst other techniques which it explores is the single-frame image, lasting only 1/24 second, which he uses in a pulsating rhythm.

This is also the first film in which the image of a film sprocket-hole is used as a conscious element in the film. The image probably originated as an accident in the hand-painting process, but was clearly taken up deliberately by Lye as a reference to the film material itself. In addition he insists that its presence should act at another level, and its rectangular shape, wandering across the frame, is taken up by a drawn 'abstract' rectangle, which in turn takes on the identity of a letter or parcel similarly moving across the screen.

All Len Lye's work of this period explores the combination of these techniques and hand-drawn film but during the war he suspended technical experiment in favour of more conventional forms working with documentary film-makers. After the war he went to the USA, only resuming his experimental film work in 1952, when he again took up the hand-made film, culminating in *Free Radicals*. None of his later work establishes significant new ground, much of his innovative energy in this period being devoted to kinetic sculpture, but the last films are a mature refinement of his hand-drawn, film calligraphy.

Len Lye and Oskar Fischinger represent the end of the pre-war period, and at the same time are part of the link with the post-war developments in America. Oskar Fischinger in particular was a major and direct influence on the emerging American situation. We should remember that Fischinger, Lye, Richter, Man Ray, and Duchamp actually moved to America, making a link through their films, and together with many other important artists who likewise fled from Europe, created an extremely lively grouping in the one western democracy which had finance enough to be really concerned about art.

Whatever the causes—money, a lively artistic atmosphere, or the adoption of 16mm in America since the last war—a new kind of film culture has gradually established itself as a viable alternative concept of cinema. This has been variously named the New American Cinema, or the Underground, and by now has been fairly well documented in a number of books. There have been at least four identifiable trends: the first is the continuation of non-figurative film; next is the continuation from the Surrealist film tradition of Buñuel and Dali, including film-makers like Maya Deren and Kenneth Anger; third is the area which best fits the title of New American Cinema, which sought to bring new forms to commercial cinema, and includes film-makers like Shirley Clarke and John Cassavetes; the last is the recent, formal movement, which is much more international, and can be seen as an extension of the search initiated by Man Ray and Léger for a 'cinematic' basis of new formal concept in film. The whole range is characterized by the idea of a 'personal' cinema, in the sense that most of the films are the product of a single person, but only the abstract film, and the new formal film, are central to this book.

# 7 · America post-war

The American abstract film movement began just a little before the start of World War II, when John Whitney and perhaps Harry Smith produced their first important work. These two remain the leading figures of the movement, which includes Jordan Belson, John Whitney's brother James, and more recently, John's three sons, John Jnr, Michael and Mark. The movement, which has largely grown up on the West Coast in the Los Angeles and San Francisco areas, should also include Hy Hirsh, though he in fact reversed the direction of migration by moving to Europe in the fifties. Other West Coast film-makers belong with the movement if only by virtue of single films, notably Pat O'Neill with *7362* (1967) and John Stehura with *Cybernetic 5.3* (1969), a computer-generated firework display. Mary Ellen Bute, and her husband Ted Nemeth, also made some abstract work, including experiments using oscilloscope images in films like *Abstronics* (1954). However, their work (which is very difficult to see) seems most closely linked to that of Norman McLaren, or, based on a tight synchronization to music, to a late continuation of the aesthetic of Fischinger, who remained a significant figure in the movement until his death in 1967.

Related to this abstract work is another direction, which uses live-action material, but explores the technological transformation of this through film printing and video techniques. This includes film-makers like Ron Nameth, Scott Bartlett, who is best known, and the main work of the less well-known but more important Pat O'Neill, to whom I shall refer later. Another film-maker who has worked in this area is Stan Vanderbeek, though he mainly works in New York.

One underlying attitude of all the artists considered so far in this book has been their intention to treat film as a 'plastic' medium. They have sought to develop the medium as an area within which 'film thought' can take place, rather than as a tool for the expression of literary ideas. The main problem of asking about meaning in this context is that most of our popular conceptions of meaning and the critical language with which we define it is derived from literary habits. In film, as in art, the organization of the elements, qualities and characteristics of the medium is a means of intelligent thought, in its own right, and we should not be surprised if the patterns of thought which we encounter via this mode are different in kind to those which derive from other media. In many ways our minds and eyes are not culturally attuned to the conditions of thinking directly through film, so we feel the need to translate that experience into a more familiar mode. Not only is the 'art' of film itself little developed in plastic terms but the critical language to deal with it is even less so. Most of the major critics of cinema have a strong literary bias, being more at home with narrative, dramatic, symbolist or sur-realist forms. Certainly, in the field of 'plastic' cinema, questions of means and meaning remain closely bound together, but some questions concerning interpretation are unavoidable, particularly in consideration of the American post-war abstract movement, and some of the more general West Coast tendencies.

There is a sense in which one would expect the non-representational direction of cinema to be that most removed from the 'psychologically expressive' intentions of the Symbolists and Surrealists, but in many ways the opposite is true. Fischinger, for example, became increasingly concerned with the 'spiritual' and 'mystical' aspects of his work, and this religious conception is one which follows through to many of the West Coast film-makers (not simply as a result of Fischinger's influence). On the West Coast, following the war, there was a steady growth of interest in Oriental religions, mystical experience, meditative practice and drug experimentation. The popularization of passive, quietist philosophies or religions, whose patterns have been established in stable, caste or feudally structured societies, is ominous when it occurs in the context of the aggressive technology of a western capitalist state like America. Its most extreme filmic expression is in the work of Scott Bartlett, backed by the criticism of Gene Youngblood.

In Bartlett's *OFFON* and *Moon '69*, an advanced plastic sensibility is used to celebrate what is in effect an imperialist technology and political structure—a dangerous and unwitting effect of artists working from a quietist, mystical philosophy. Remember that Leni Riefenstahl had a similarly developed filmic sensibility. However, in discussing Bartlett, Youngblood seems completely unaware of this. In his description of *Moon '69* he says:

> *Moon* begins in a black void as we hear a recording of the Apollo Eight astronauts reading from Genesis. Under this is a rather spacey track from the Steve Miller album, *Sailor*. Suddenly the black void is recognized as a night sky as we approach a distant airport whose lights seem to float in deep space. The image is flopped; the runway lights become a starry corridor similar to the slit-scan corridor of *2001*. This gives way to stop-frame, optically distorted footage of astronauts boarding their craft before takeoff. The pale colors and unearthly motions lend a kind of dreamlike *déjà-vu* quality to the scene as these hooded creatures lumber slowly towards the giant rocket.[1]

Youngblood's style of criticism colludes with the film's naïve optimism about technology. Technology is not apolitical!

However, these strictures do not apply equally to all the West Coast work, neither do they imply that all approach to film or art from a 'spiritual' or 'meditative' standpoint is intrinsically suspect. Many artists have sought to express their ideas on art in metaphysical terms, particularly Eggeling and Kandinsky who form a major background to the abstract film movement. In many respects, the connection between the American abstract films of this period and Kandinsky's art and theory should be developed. Not only does Kandinsky express a similar, basically religious attitude to art, but there is a direct similarity in the aesthetic factors of his paintings to much of the abstract film of this period. A fundamental link between most abstract film and Kandinsky rests on the assumption that abstract forms and colour contain intrinsic meanings. This is not in the sense of literary symbolism—the basis of Freudian interpretation of visual symbols as object—word archetypal structures, with which literary critics feel so at home—but more related to the Jungian conception of archetypal form.

Wassily Kandinsky: *Battle*, 1910

In *Concerning the Spiritual in Art*, Kandinsky attempts to deal with the creative process as a whole, and in particular the way in which decisions in art are based on 'inner necessity'. In many respects this is nothing other than the development of a sense of 'rightness' by the artist, which can guide his artistic construction and choice. In Kandinsky's view, this sensibility can be trained (self-trained) as an 'exercise of the spirit'. He gives as the starting-point for this exercise the study of colour and its effects, the first being physical—the registration of sensation—and the second psychological, of which he says:

> [Colours] produce a correspondent spiritual vibration, and it is only as a step towards this spiritual vibration that the physical impression is of importance.
> Whether the psychological effect of colour is direct as these last few lines imply, or whether it is the outcome of association, is open to question. The soul being one with the body, it may well be possible that a psychological tremor generates a corresponding one through association.

Kandinsky applies similar conceptions to the experience of forms. It is because he attempts to trace the process from the physical to the metaphysical, that even if we reject his religiosity, many aspects of his conception remain useful. Most artists who would reject much of Kandinsky's metaphysics still implicitly make their artistic decisions on the basis of interior impulse, a sense of 'rightness' corresponding closely to Kandinsky's concept of 'inner necessity'. Because he admits that

Harry Smith: *Film Number 3*, before 1950

'innate' reaction to colour or form may be the result of association, the 'archetypal' requires no more mystical explanation than consistencies in our environment and experience. At the lower level, the link between the physical and psychological effects of colour or form, he still draws a clear relationship between the material aspects of a work and its 'meaning'.

In formal terms, Kandinsky's work did most to prefigure sequential abstract animation by his frequent use of phased repetition of clearly similar elements. Kandinsky's work not only explores the notion of shape transformation, or colour changes within repeated shapes, but also shape repetitions which imply movement either across the surface or into the 'space' of the picture. Even the abstract films of the early period can be thought of within this tradition, but with the introduction of colour into film the relationship becomes very strong. Though the whole abstract film movement after the war can be seen in relationship to Kandinsky's aesthetics, the clearest visual link is in the films of Harry Smith.

Smith had begun working with film before 1940, but in his case there can be no certainty about the dating of his earliest work. Not only is his deepest concern with myth, but this has extended to deliberately encouraging a mystique about his own life and work.[2] The literary aspect of myth and symbolism has gradually become dominant in his work, his purely abstract films all being made approximately in the period before 1950. These are numbered 1 to 7, and it is only these films which are of interest in the present context. As with both Ruttmann and Fischinger, we can see a broad pattern of development to the films, which begins with an anthropomorphic stage and moves through a dominantly geo-metric mode towards an optical dynamic. He began work unaware of other experiments in abstract film. He later encountered the work of Lye, has specifically acknowledged a debt to the Whitneys in a theoretical and technical sense and one film is actually dedicated to Oskar Fischinger.

In *Numbers 1, 2* and *3* he developed the most accomplished technique to date in the genre of the hand-made film. Working on 35mm, he came to achieve a precision of registration in his third film which often makes it difficult to realize that the film is not photographed as con-ventional animation. His method in these films has been reasonably described as 'batik', in which he applied razor-cut masking-tape or manufactured gummed circles to areas of the frame and then sprayed it with colour. The coloured areas were then treated with a protective resist like vaseline, the masks removed and the resulting unprotected areas sprayed in. Much of the 'jitter' and frenetic pace of the hand-made film was eliminated by this laborious technique. Smith reports working for up to five years on *Number 3* but the spray method of applying colour allowed smooth gradations and a great tonal richness. In *Numbers 4, 5* and *7* (*Number 6*, reported as a 3-D experiment no longer seems to exist) Smith continued the formal direction of the batiked films but using a simpler and more conventional, photographic technique. He gradually increased the use of layered superimposition of his moving geometric forms, but motion was achieved by camera movement and the zoom rather than by the animation of visual elements before a static camera. In this way he explored complement and counter-point, the changing scales and movements of simple geometric forms superimposed on one another.

His most complex abstract film, *Number 7*, explores the refilming of black and white forms projected through changing colour filters, and it is in this film that ground and figure begin to approach equality. One basic difference between Kandinsky-esque abstraction and the develop-ment from it of an optical dynamic is in the relationship of figure to ground. As geometric abstraction emerged from 'landscape' space, geometric figures replaced objects like trees, houses or people, but the picture surface on which they appeared was still conceived similarly to sea, earth, sky or a stellar space. A change from this figure/ground interpretation only comes about when both areas achieve an equivalence of scale, so that the relationship gives way to total optical surface. It is at the point when the visual elements have equal 'value' that geometric abstraction gives way to an optical dynamic. We see some equivalent of this shift in Ruttmann's last abstract film, the late work of Fischinger, and some hint of it in sections of Harry Smith's *Number 7*. However, Smith does not complete the transition, mainly because what his work sought (or seeks) is a form which does differentiate figure from ground, a necessary condition for his symbolist direction.

Where Smith has returned to figurative symbolism, John Whitney pursues a consistent abstract project. Particularly up to 1944 John Whitney worked closely with his younger brother James, but John has remained the more committed to film as his medium and is certainly the greater technical innovator. He began his abstract film experiments on 8mm during 1939 in Paris, having absolutely no awareness of earlier work of this kind. He describes his major artistic influence at that time as having been Schönberg via a deep friendship with the conductor and Schönberg devotee, René Liebowitz, but, soon after his return to the USA in 1940, he also encountered Fischinger and Man Ray.

Almost at once Whitney became aware that the images he could make and the way they behaved were directly related to the techniques he could invent. Even with the early 8mm work, he began to apply an exceptional talent for mechanical invention to his film production; in an interview[3] he describes how he had begun by preparing large numbers of file cards on which he had stencilled shapes, using an air-brush, then filmed this bank of gradually changing shapes on black and white film stock. He goes on to say: 'I built an 8mm optical printer, so that I could rephotograph those sequences according to a carefully worked out script, introducing colour filters into the light source and photographing the sequences onto colour film.' He then explains how he was still using this basic technique in adding colour to his recent computer-generated films. Not only has it become a standard procedure for him, it is also central to much of the later work exploring image trans-formation through printing. Although it relates to the techniques employed by Fischinger and Lye in their use of Gasparcolour, where the basic material is also black and white, Whitney's process was made possible by the development of colour-sensitive emulsions allowing a simpler photographic process.

Intrinsic to his technique at this and every other stage is the idea of permutating the relationships of basic image units, most clearly realized in the *Five Film Exercises* (1943–4) made with his brother. For this series, John also made the most interesting contribution to date to the experiments with synthetic optical sound, for which he constructed a system of interconnected pendula. Their various movements and counter-movements were transmitted mechanically by a common wire, called a 'wiffle-tree', to an aperture in the camera which opened and closed in response to the combined movement to create a pattern on an optical

John and James Whitney: from *Five Film Exercises*, 1943–44, showing original synthetic optical soundtrack

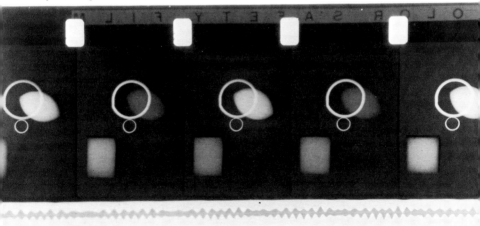

soundtrack. This was then synchronized with the images, and in spite of its primitive quality is probably the most satisfactory combination of image and sound in the field of the non-figurative film.

John Whitney continued to experiment with new techniques for creating the image on film, but his most significant move was to experiment with computer systems. Using war surplus anti-aircraft gun directors in 1957 he began the construction of an animation table, which allowed sections to rotate according to pre-programmed patterns, transforming very simple visual forms into complex movements similar to oscilloscope or pendulum-pantograph figures. The most exciting abstract work from this system is *Lapis*, made by James between 1963 and 1966 on a similar system which John constructed for him. Furthermore it is the best example of a meditative film-mandala made in the West Coast ethos. However one sees the cause, the technological direction which John Whitney explored during this period had a tendency to generate forms which suited centre-orientated, meditational intentions. The mandala recurs frequently in all the Whitneys' work, John taking this form up strongly in his first film generated with an IBM digital computer, *Permutations* (1968).

John Whitney's theoretical considerations have mostly centred around the analogies between film structure and music or language. Many of his statements are prefaced by an assertion; similar to that expressed by Fischinger, that film, as an abstract medium, is at a primitive level of development in comparison with music. Through his adoption of the digital computer, within the genre of abstract film, Whitney has done most to point a way out of the dominance of Kandinsky's aesthetic over abstract cinema. The factor which particularly challenges Kandinsky stems almost directly from the computer capability, though it also emerges as a new aesthetic direction in work not related to computers. This is the permutation principle and its 'programmability'. As with Robert Breer, who also began to explore permutation of his animation images, Whitney encounters the 'arbitrary' or the 'alternative'—challenging the search for a single, right fusion based on 'inner necessity'.

Although the digital computer is ideally suited to programmed permutation, exploring variations of a limited set of visual units, surprisingly none of his computer films have fully developed this aspect. They continue to point a direction without fulfilling it, and are still held in the pull of conflicting aesthetic directions. Whitney, like all the other exponents of 'computer film', Stan Vanderbeek, John Stehura and Lillian Schwartz for example, mostly uses the computer only to produce isolated sequences of abstract imagery which are then later combined and transformed according to aesthetic principles at variance with the intrinsic capacities of the computer. With the early influence of Schönberg, it is surprising that Whitney does not see how the serialist conception of structure is more advanced than the dominating aesthetic of his computer films, as well as providing a more appropriate basis for a mathematical and programmed artistic form.

In spite of this criticism, John Whitney's digital computer films are the clearest and most satisfactory work in this field to date, the most appropriate to the computer process being the simplest: an unedited, black-and-white, time 'sculpture' called *1-2-3* (1970).

James Whitney: *Lapis*, 1963–66

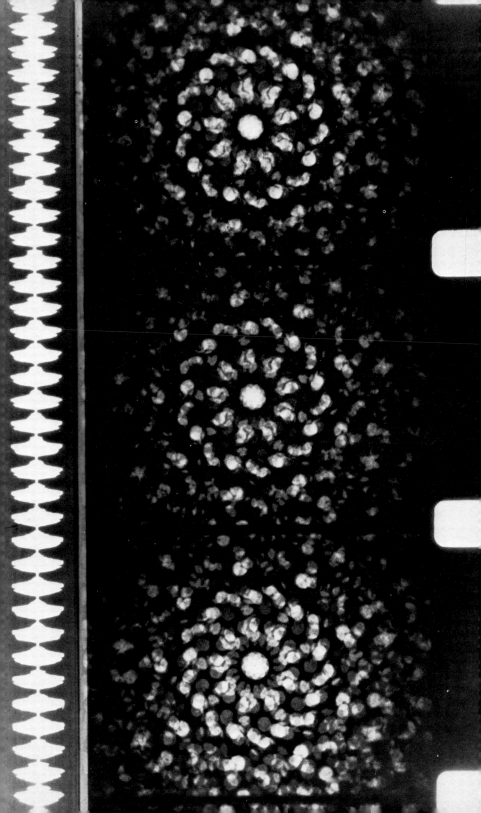

at another they maintain all the worst aspects of illusionist cinema, almost demanding an associative mode of interpretation, a tendency which is further encouraged by wistful and ill-conceived electronic montage soundtracks.

In particular, the soundtracks do much, especially in *World* (1970) and *Cosmos* (1971), to reinforce a mood of nostalgia. Here again the similarity with science fiction emerges, as the nostalgia is inverted, its object not an unrecoverable past, but an unattainable future. Of course, passage through his cosmological or molecular imagery is seen as an analogue for that through interior states of consciousness in the Buddhist sense, but even as such the element of nostalgia, now for an unattainable or lost purity and perfection, still pervades the work. This shows the schism of Belson in a more fundamental philosophical light. The language of the modern art tradition to which he relates is one which is based on the physical and existential. This relates to a philosophy which since Hegel has increasingly banished transcendental concepts and other-worldly religious heavens, seeing life and experience as, however varied in state, essentially finite and physical. Belson's work seems an attempt to reinstate the transcendental, a purpose at odds with the concrete basis of the aesthetic tradition to which he belongs. If, on the other hand, his purpose is not transcendental, but seeks to explore the physical aspect of transformation, albeit mental or psychological, then his film language is open to misinterpretation.

Of the other film-makers who have contributed to this movement, Hy Hirsh is the most interesting and probably the most neglected. He died in 1960 and had taken little care of his films, which are consequently difficult to find and see. His work is not consistently abstract in the non-figurative sense, but like *Couleur de la Forme* (1952), which is made from reflection textures in water, he often filmed unidentifiable objects or surfaces in close-up, sometimes reprinting them with colour filters which further obscures the identity of the original material. A friend of Harry Smith, and a contributor to the Vortex concerts before leaving America for Europe, he was an influential figure in the loose grouping of film-makers which included the Whitneys and Belson. His best abstract film I have seen is *Eneri*, which may have been made at any time between 1955 and 1958, and is one of the few films to survive intact with the original soundtrack. Based mainly on oscilloscope patterns, but also using abstracted live-action images, it employs complex split-screen printing so that many abstract developments are shown at different scales simultaneously—not in superimposition, but split up within the single frame. Perhaps when all his work is collected, and to some extent restored, Hirsh will emerge as a much more important figure in this movement.

The direction of film abstraction begun by artists like Eggeling and Ruttmann continues especially through the Whitneys. However, in recent years, involvement in film at a plastic and formal level has tended to swing strongly away from this direction. This swing could be seen, like the work of Léger and Man Ray, as a search for a more cinematic development of film form. I have already suggested that the abstract films of the twenties in a way counteracted the dominance over film form by theatre and literature with a dominance by painting and perhaps

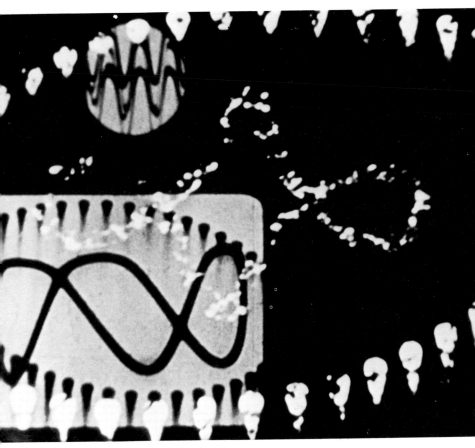

Hy Hirsh: *Eneri*, 1955–58

music. Although in abstract cinema the camera is used to record the
abstract images, the essentially photographic potential of film is largely
redundant, and any method for establishing the images on the celluloid
would suffice.

This swing could also be understood in another way. Much of the
post-war work in abstract cinema is relatable to the aesthetics of
Kandinsky. Other painters, like Malevitch, could have been mentioned,
but they would all have belonged to a similar historical period. The
particular aesthetic issues of that form of painting are no longer relevant
as contemporary art but, at the same time, the work of Frank Stella,
Jasper Johns, or subsequent movements like Land, Concept or Body
Art, are all dependent on the historical fact of the 'abstract' tradition. In
this respect, recent tendencies in formal cinema which I shall deal with
next can be seen as part of the same tradition as 'abstract' cinema, but
like the more recent developments in painting or sculpture, are aesthetically more advanced.

# 8 · Beginnings of the new formal film

Missing out most of the continuity represented by what is known as the underground film, I shall now take up the development of the new formal cinema. For this area, though I would wish it otherwise, P. Adams Sitney's designation 'structural film' has stuck, in much the same way that the critics' reaction to the planar simplicity of certain pictures by Braque and Picasso left us with the equally inadequate term Cubism. If there is a connection between structuralism as it is applied in cinema and as it has come to be applied in anthropology, linguistics or economics, it is not a simple, obvious connection. I have little doubt that Sitney's original use of the term[1] was somewhat fortuitous and did not stem from any deeply reasoned connection with other branches of structuralism. Though others have tried to formulate some connection, and it is possible to find some parallels, Sitney never seems to have been bothered by this arbitrariness enough to try to clear it up. The other major inadequacy inherent in Sitney's use of the term is that the work which he includes is so varied that it makes nonsense of his categorization.

Where it helps to create a critical grasp, I shall refer to structuralism. I am not altogether happy with the term 'formal' film, but it has the virtue of being more general, and is not so loaded with the misconceptions which derive from Sitney's unsatisfactory designation. In *Visionary Film*, he tries to distinguish between the formal and the structural film as follows:

> The formal film is a tight nexus of context, a shape designed to explore the facets of the material . . . Recurrences, prolepses, antitheses, and overall rhythms are the rhetoric of the formal . . .
> The structural film insists on its shape, and what content it has is minimal and subsidiary to the outline. Four characteristics of the structural film are its fixed camera position (fixed frame from the viewer's perspective), the flicker effect, loop printing, and rephotography off the screen.

This is simplistic and confusing. During the sixties, and particularly after 1966, many films explored these devices. For example *Tom Tom the Piper's Son* (1969) by Ken Jacobs, is defined as structural, though it could also fit exactly his own definition of formal—'a shape designed to explore the facets of the material'. For Sitney, Michael Snow is the dean of structural film-makers, and certain aspects of his work, particularly in ←→ (1969) and *The Central Region* (1971), can be usefully examined in relation to the general field of structuralism, but not for the reasons Sitney quotes. For him, the structuralism of Snow's films rests essentially on their simplified, overall shape, but this concept of shape is no more than one form for the unification of content, especially in *Wavelength* (1967), the film which probably did most to establish 'shape' as a major determinant of the structural category. If structuralism is to be usefully applied, it must be in terms of structuralist activity or process. The relationship between the camera procedure in both ←→ and *The Central*

*Region* and its effect on the modelling of spatial experience could usefully be pursued as a 'structural' problem. But the loose concept of shape is of little help. He is right in so far as there is a tendency, and there are definable characteristics or regions of cinematic inquiry within the tendency, but his misleading and premature application of the term 'structural' actually obscures analysis of the various developments.

To understand Sitney's conception, it is necessary to compare the context from which the formal tendency emerged in America with the way in which a similar tendency emerged in Europe. It is essential to see the extent to which the mainstream of New American Cinema—Maya Deren, James Broughton, Sidney Peterson, Kenneth Anger, Gregory Markopoulos, Jack Smith, Ron Rice, Stan Brakhage, Bruce Baillie and so forth—is embedded in a Romantic, Symbolist, Expressionist tradition, with the roots of its cinematic form in Surrealist cinema. In spite of the West Coast abstract school, the formal aspects of abstraction made only small impact—and even this abstract school is strongly dominated by the same Romantic and Symbolist forces, illustrated by the later work of Harry Smith and Jordan Belson.

For the European film-makers who became allied to the underground film movement mostly during the late sixties, the predominance of this Romantic tradition has only recently become apparent. For them (certainly for many of the British film-makers) what was important about the work of the underground and New American Cinema was that it seemed to share their own concern with establishing new formal principles for cinema. For the resident European, where, for a couple of centuries, space and resources have become increasingly scarce, and in the last sixty years the population has experienced the tensions of extreme political conflicts and been torn apart by two major wars, a-political Romanticism holds singularly little intellectual credence. As in politics and economics, problems in modern European art have always been 'tight' problems, with little sense of a vast range of alternatives. It is possible that the shift towards formalism in the recent American avant-garde film reflects some of the dawning awareness in the USA that it also has real political and economic constraints to which the 'frontier' mentality no longer supplies a credible solution, though the psychological attitudes seem to persist. America now begins to face the problems of constrained social relationships from which many of its population 'historically' fled when they first left Europe.

Whatever the cause, when experiment with film as a medium of plastic art re-emerged in Europe following the Second World War, about fifteen to twenty years later than in America, its bias was largely formal. Even where it was expressionist, as with many of the films which grew out of the Austrian Direct Art movement, it was strongly anti-Romantic and clearly based in the psycho-physical as material phenomena. It is from this frame of reference that some of the dominant characteristics of the New American Cinema or underground film were misread in Europe.

Whilst the shift to formal concerns in the American avant-garde took place in the context of a well-developed Symbolist tradition of underground cinema in Europe the formal tendency emerged first, encountering the underground tradition in the mid- and late sixties. However, even if the American underground work was Romantic, it still represented undeniable advances in cinematic convention and language, advances built into the culture through realized works and not just changes in theory or attitude. They were the result of almost twenty years' independent experiment at a time when very little was taking place in this field in a Europe slowly recovering from almost total economic disruption during and after the war. As real advances in the conventions of cinema, they could not be avoided or dismissed. There were also evident formal parallels with areas which European film-makers had begun to explore.

Yet the bias of the 'dialectic' between formal inclinations and the underground tradition was different in Europe to America. So, whilst the American underground has had an undeniable influence on contemporary European film-makers, the formal direction of much recent European work was already initiated before the American influence, and certainly before Sitney's American structuralists were heard of in Europe. In many respects, the formal bias of post-war European work can be considered as a continuation of the search for new cinematic form begun in the twenties, even though it was not a direct reaction to the films themselves which, like the American underground films, were not seen until the new movement was underway.

In America the formal inclination was initially a reaction against the underground film, particularly in the work of Warhol whose intentions were not expressly formal but rather initiated as a provocative, neo-Dada reaction. In Europe it was a striving for new cinematic form in a vacuum, referring more to other areas of art than cinema.

In tracing the development of this new formal tendency, I shall accept the broad divergence of the experimentation, and instead of seeing those factors which Sitney refers to, like flicker effect, loop printing, and re-photography, as identifying characteristics of a category, I shall see them as concerns or directions of inquiry in a broad formal tendency. I shall add to them a number of other concerns, like celluloid as material, the projection as event, duration as a concrete dimension. I shall also modify Sitney's characteristic of the fixed camera in favour of a more general exploration of camera-functioning and the consequences of camera-motion or procedure in their various forms. I shall refer generally to the question of procedure as a determinant of form.

Until the period 1966–1968, in which the new formal issues emerged in a number of works isolating them more clearly, there were two Americans, Stan Brakhage and Andy Warhol, and two Austrians, Kurt Kren and Peter Kubelka, who form the major background of this tendency.

Brakhage's work in the American underground film represents its most radical break with the aims and aspirations of commercial cinema. It is rightly understood as epitomizing the direction of personal, visionary cinema, establishing, more than any other film-maker's, the camera as heroic protagonist. Though his earliest films clearly relate to a narrative, Surrealist tradition, it is quickly apparent that his use of the camera is significantly different to that of any film-maker before him. This is not just a question of style, but more fundamental. Brakhage begins to concentrate the major expressive means in the camera action itself: it is not simply a matter of using a hand-held camera; it is a more thorough realization that the camera is not a neutral observer of action, but an active participant.

Even the greater mobility and increased use of natural locations in the commercial cinéma verité movement never realize the camera as the essential 'first person' of cinema. Dziga Vertov established the 'idea' of the camera as participant, but his references to it were more literary than plastic, via film of a camera in use, taken by another camera which itself maintained a basic 'neutrality'. The conception of the camera and cinema which emerges from Brakhage represents a fundamental shift in awareness. Brakhage appears to create a polarity between objective and subjective cinema, but what he actually achieves is an awareness that there can be no alternative to the camera's subjective role. In commercial cinema the false neutrality of the camera is a major cause of its aesthetic and philosophical retardation, its attitude being parallel to the viewpoint of the novelist in the Victorian novel.

The relationship drawn by Sitney between Brakhage and the Abstract Expressionist painters is reasonable. Brakhage is primarily an Expressionist, more concerned with utilizing subjective means towards expressing a personal vision than with clarifying the nature of his process (at least within the films themselves rather than in his writing). Therefore, Brakhage never develops his initial innovation in attitude to the camera towards more precise limitations of its mode of functioning, though he comes close to it in *Sirius Remembered* (1959), prefiguring work by Snow and Gidal. This, more than any of his other films, points the way for the extension of his camera aesthetic in a direction which his own Expressionist attitude never allows him to follow.

The film unwittingly highlights the duality between its Romantic Expressionist content—the dead and decaying family dog—and its formal, choreographic camerawork, which never allows involvement in the image, but creates a distance from it, almost establishing a super-imposed observation system. What would otherwise be emotionally loaded images become no more than points of visual reference in the repetition of vertical and horizontal camera movements. However, it never overcomes the lack of synthesis between Brakhage's Romantic motivation as embodied in the ostensible subject (the rotting dog) and the camera action. The value system implied by the Romantic Symbolism is challenged by the physical kinetics of the camera. It is a similar incompatibility to that seen in the earliest paintings of Cézanne where the observational 'method' conflicted with the Symbolist pictorial elements, like skulls and handless clocks. Cézanne resolved this by the use of subject matter which avoided symbolic, emotional loading and allowed the transfer of attention entirely to the observational relations.

Though not as far-reaching as his fundamental innovation in assumptions about the camera, there are two other areas to which Brakhage has contributed. The first is in the genre of the hand-made film, and the second is that of permutative film construction. In neither can he be seen as a sole innovator, but in the hand-made film, through *Mothlight* (1963) and the mould-growth on *Song 14* (1965), he shifts this approach to film further towards an awareness of the material aspects of film as the basis of 'content'. In a number of his works, he has made marks by hand, but these have generally been thought of as sequential calligraphic addition to the images. In *Mothlight* and *Song 14*, the projected image was an unpredictable result of the action on the material. *Mothlight* was made by the direct collage of flower petals, moth wings, grass and thin stalks onto the 16mm film strip. The image was printed for preservation and projection, but the material qualities are strong in the image, occupying the very shallow visual space defined by the thickness of film in a projector gate. The physical problem of making a printable collage, which also allowed the passage of light through the surface, determined that the objects used should be thin or translucent. This makes them a metaphor for the nature of the celluloid on which they are supported, the implied depth of the image being the material depth of the object and the celluloid. The mould-growth on sections of the 8mm *Song 14* establishes a similar shallow material space, but at the same time raises questions of another order, involving attention to the chemical nature of cinematic process, an issue recently taken up more directly by Tony Conrad. Both films point to the material aspects of film in a way which is precluded when action on the celluloid is directed towards the sequential animation of graphic images.

As an editor, at an abstract level, Brakhage continues the historical development of montage relationships based on shape, motion and colour similarities, and counterpoint. He also continues the development of editing pulse, interchanging images with each other or with clear or colour spacing. At the level of image association he develops a form of Joycean stream of consciousness, using rapid intercutting to establish a 'cluster' form of psycho-montage, an extension from Surrealist form. Without diminishing his achievement in this field, this direction for editing must be seen to have been latent in the culture which Brakhage inherited, the direction having already been initiated by the avant-garde work of the twenties, both formal and Surrealist. Where he begins to see a new perspective for this form is in his epic-scale *Art of Vision* (completed in 1965; lasting 4½ hours). Brakhage's essential artistic process is one of impulsive selection and construction, never constraining himself by preconception of didactic procedure. This process is very similar to Abstract Expressionism, and, like it, is concerned with materializing psycho-associative relationships, strongly biased towards bodily rather than literary analogies. Structure or form in this kind of process is not *a priori*, but the result of a search for 'a logic' during the selection and construction process.

In the *Art of Vision*, Brakhage's first long film, he tries to establish a form strong enough to sustain the intricate immediacy of his cluster-type montage over the very long time-scale. The method used is the permutative superimposition of edited sequences of equal length, which, for most of the film, are six or nine minutes long. In each of the sections, once the sequences have been edited, their only further development is in their superimpositions upon each other. In the final section, for example, four six-minute, tightly edited sequences permutate all their combinations of superimposition, first all four together, then the combinations of three, the six combinations of two, ending with the presentation of each in turn. An important result of this form is that it allows passive involvement in Brakhage's personal universe, but at the same time permits a critical distance for the audience due to the flexible arbitrariness of the permutated relationships. It allows the audience to participate in the construction of relationships, rather than being restricted to an entirely passive response. But perhaps more important for the film-maker, it reveals the arbitrary nature of his own associative system, and its

Stan Brakhage: *Mothlight*, 1963

Andy Warhol: *Harlot*, 1965

dependence on the film form which is available. If it is assumed that the aim of cinematic convention is a single unification of material, then this imposes that mode of conception on the film-maker. If a film form can be developed which allows alternative relationships of content, then this leads to new conceptions about the nature of experience, since how we think about the world depends on the conventions we can create to model it.

Where Brakhage's formal innovations are the result of a linear development of his film aesthetic, Andy Warhol's were very much a reaction against the existing film culture and particularly the Romantic underground ethos, including Brakhage. Warhol's role in the formal cinema is rather curious, for whilst certain aspects of his innovations are as fundamental as Brakhage's change in the basic concept of camera, in many respects he seems not to have grasped their implications. Warhol has always been more concerned with impact than form—formal innovation being a by-product of impact. He is essentially a neo-Dadaist attempting to provoke response, and using his media, including film, primarily to propagate attitudes. As we have seen with Man Ray, formal innovation can derive from Dadaist intention. The process is not so difficult to understand: fundamental assaults on habitual preconceptions necessarily create a formal vacuum—extreme rejection of established conventions, even as an end in itself, makes way for the acceptance only of that which is not contained in the old form. His early films—those made during his initial rejection of established cinematic convention—contain his most significant contribution. Since this period he has become more and more a producer in the accepted sense, lending his name to narrative action films by inferior directors like Paul Morrisey.

In Warhol's *Sleep* (1963) Sitney identifies three of his four characteristics of structural film—only flicker effect is absent. Of these, he pays most attention to the fixed camera frame, referring to the notion of the long stare, but he also identifies the repetition of $2\frac{3}{4}$-minute takes as a loop printing device, and a single frame freeze as being equivalent to the later technique of refilming from the screen. The last two observations are tenuous as the repetition of long sequences of action have a different function and experience to the rhythmic and fairly rapid repetitions of an actual film-loop, and they should be considered as separate formal devices. In the same way, the mechanically printed freeze-frame has quite different implications to the transformational function of refilming. However, the fixed camera and fixed frame are rightly understood in terms of concentrating attention—the fixed stare (a critical observation first made by Peter Gidal in 1971). They should also be understood as showing the inevitable limitation and selection caused by the very act of filming, expressed through the 'cut-off' of the film frame.

Perhaps the single most important formal issue in Warhol's early films is that of duration, in terms of which all three of the devices referred to by Sitney can be understood. Not simply a question of a film's length, it involves a concept of the time dimension of film as 'concrete', requiring that the film should be experienced as an actual passage of time. This is not an automatic or 'normal' state of affairs in film, either in the commercial cinema or even in avant-garde work. Narrative structure in cinema has been consistently developed towards the opposite end—that of constructing illusory time. Indeed the photographic aspect of cinema is not its main basis of illusion. As a direct physico-chemical extension from the events which it records, the photographic aspect of cinematography should be considered as a material rather than an illusionist factor.

The main basis of illusion in cinema stems from the manipulation of time and space relationships between shots. The editing concept which dominated underground cinema up to Warhol largely sought to eliminate time relationships in the narrative sense in favour of a non-temporal concept of interrelationships. As a development from film Surrealism, particularly with Brakhage, the notion of montage was taken to the extreme degree of having the sequential path through images represent simultaneous association. As in Joyce's *Finnegans Wake*, the sequential development of a work does not seek to represent consequential events in the world, but traces paths through a psycho-associative matrix of relationships, representing a non-temporal mental state. This 'associative matrix' concept of montage relates closely to the distinction made by Maya Deren between 'vertical' as opposed to 'horizontal' development.[2] By 'horizontal' she simply meant the consequent development of action or narrative, whilst by 'vertical' she implied a cross-section of mental experience or images which associate to a non-temporal idea or state. In Brakhage's *Art of Vision*, this concept, though essentially non-temporal, is extended over an extremely long period, and it leads to an experience of the film's actual duration. This is simply a result of prolonged exposure to the non-narrative form. But in it, as in Von Stroheim's *Greed* (1923) or Wagner's *Ring*, the durational experience becomes attached to the awe-inspiring epic intent.

Warhol exploited an almost opposite device: he showed that experience of duration as a concrete dimension could be achieved simply by the prolonged exposure to long periods of inactivity, and, by relating it to the commonplace, robbed it of any romantic epic implications. Whatever Warhol's intention (and the suspicion remains that he was more concerned with provocation than the refinement of durational sensibility), his contribution in this area goes beyond simple provocative exposure to long periods of minimal change, as in *Empire* (1964), an 8-hour film of the Empire State Building from a fixed position. This kind of exposure inevitably results in a breakdown of involvement in the film. Attention unavoidably moves 'out' of the film to awareness of its physical context and the current time and space of its presentation—a functional boredom.

But in Warhol we also discover the value of a new cinematic concept, that of representational equivalence in duration. In most of his early films, like *Sleep, Kiss, Couch* (both 1964) or *Harlot* (1965), each take is the length of a single roll of film, which, depending on the type of camera, is either $2\frac{3}{4}$ or 11 minutes long, and these are simply strung together in sequence. Experience of the film's length can be used as a direct analogue for the film's interior duration, that of its minimal action. This analogue is made possible by the nearly one-to-one equivalence between the length of the filming and the screening. In a form of cinema based on confrontation with the material aspects of the medium this unbroken, durational equivalence provides the only counteract to illusion in the representation of time.

There are very few instances in commercial cinema, or even documentary cinema, where the film's length equals the duration of its action. For example, in Agnes Varda's *Cleo from 5 to 7* (1961), the film's actual duration gets close to an equivalence for the duration of the implied action. Yet the filmic construction, the editing together of various camera set ups, betray that the equivalence is not with the material duration of the shooting, but only with the narrative duration—the implied period of action. It is much more normal for the actual length of a film to be so unrelatable to the time-span of its action that experience of the material aspect of duration becomes quite impossible.

In avant-garde film from Warhol onwards a film's screening duration may be equivalent to, or, through freezing, slowing, or repeating action, may even exceed the duration of its interior action. In Warhol, this interior action is not an implied action, even where actors are used, but a material action, recorded without reconstruction. This new awareness of film's primary dimension, that of time, can be seen as equivalent to the abandonment of deep, illusory perspective in painting, in favour of a shallow picture space, directly relatable to the material nature of the actual canvas surface. Early Warhol films establish a 'shallow' time which permits a credible relationship between the time of interior action and the physical experience of the film as a material presentation. This is Warhol's most significant innovation.

Americans other than Warhol and Brakhage have contributed to the subsequent formal developments. Gregory Markopoulos and Bruce Baillie, like Brakhage, underwent some shift to formal issues as a consequence of their own narrative, mythic or poetic directions. Bruce Connor, with *A Movie* (1958) and *Cosmic Ray* (1962), through his montage of found footage, stock shots and numbered film leader, and in spite of his associative montage construction, contributed to the concept of films as physical material. Robert Breer, in his awareness of the single frame and alternative organization of his animation images, also contributed, but the best examples of this are in his recent films, *69* (1969), *70* (1970) and *Gulls and Buoys* (1972) and a subsequent work based on animating redrawn images of an 8mm film shot from a train in Japan.

In Europe emergence of the formal direction is evident in the first works produced by almost all of the film-makers who began before the influx of American work. As the whole development of a new independent cinema was held back by economic conditions, the majority of these film-makers, Ernst Schmidt Jnr, Klaus Schonherr, Birgit and Wilhelm Hein, Peter Gidal, Peter Weibel, Werner Nekes, Lutz Mommartz, Dieter Meir, Hans Scheugl and myself, did not begin to produce work until around 1965–6 when similar directions emerged in the USA. But in Vienna, the most active centre at the beginning of the European movement, three film-makers, Peter Kubelka, Kurt Kren and Marc Adrian, were all producing work in the late fifties and early sixties. With these film-makers, especially Kubelka and Kren, it is less accurate to see them as precursors of a new formal direction, than as the first exponents of it.

Peter Kubelka has the distinction of enjoying a major reputation based on the production of only five films, all completed between 1955 and 1966, lasting in total only 38 minutes. However, there can be no doubt that in the three shortest of these works he makes a significant contribution to the new formal film. The most important of these is *Arnulf Rainer* (1960) but the two earlier works, *Adebar* (1957) and *Schwechater* (1958), represent a high point in a particular cinematic direction.

These two films are very similar in their formal conception. Both are extremely compressed graphic film poems, based on the editing of a complex rhythm of very short sequences of 'live' action film, often the interchange of single frames. The component images are reduced to an abstract graphic simplicity by the use of either the negative or high-contrast positive. In *Adebar*, there are also sequences of arrested movement—freeze frames. In these films the two major types of abstract kinetic, that based on the internal motion of pictorial elements, and that based on the rhythmic pulse of image interchange, reach a peak of aesthetic fusion, complementing each other. If Kubelka's requirement that each short film (each about one minute in length) is repeated a number of times at a single viewing is fulfilled, it is not only possible to experience the rhythm of the work, but the means of its achievement becomes clear.

These works fulfil an aesthetic direction implicit in the earliest avant-garde films because, whether or not Kubelka was aware of it at the time of making, the search in this direction was begun in Léger's *Ballet Mécanique* and clarified further in Richter's *Film Study*, particularly in its negative–positive hammer sequence. It was also clearly prefigured in the single-frame interchanges of Vertov's *Man with the Movie Camera* and Lye's *Trade Tattoo*. In both *Adebar* and *Schwechater* there is also a very satisfactory fusion of sound and image, both working within the same graphic conception.

If these two films are mostly consummation, there can be no doubt about the innovative nature of his next film, *Arnulf Rainer*, where Kubelka took the extreme step of eliminating any kind of image, representational or abstract. Other films before had made use of blank film between shots, and other films had shown some effect of flicker from image to image, but this was the first film to function solely on the interchange between black and white frames. It is thus the first wholly concrete film, and a forceful indication of the independence of cinematic abstraction from painterly abstraction in that it works with the abstraction of time change, and not with the transformation of painterly shapes. Though it prefigures the flicker film, it is not strictly a flicker film in itself, as its main concern is not retinal or related to stroboscopic effects—these are by-products. Rather it is a constructivist work, a visual music that develops a pattern of relationships between the periods of black screen and those of white counterpointed by the soundtrack, lengths of white noise and silence. As with *Adebar* and *Schwechater*, the main experience in viewing the film is perception of the pattern and rhythm of change. However, the basic nature of its means also strongly establishes the material conception of the screen and its illumination, another issue taken up by film-makers more recently.

Kubelka's reputation outside Europe is vast compared with that of his fellow Austrian Kurt Kren. But for European film-makers the work of Kren has had a more significant influence. Unlike Kubelka, who has spent much of his time in the USA, Kren remained in Europe and has made films consistently since 1957, to date completing about thirty 16mm works. Again compared with Kubelka, his work is more involved and varied, initiating a wider variety of formal issues and basic philosophical questions. There are broadly three phases in his work. The first is highly systemic; the second, beginning about 1964, is no less formal, but works in relationship to the Material-Actions of Otto Muehl and Gunter Brus, bringing a new set of issues not easily relatable to his formal notions; and the third starts around 1967, where the formal notions are again dominant but often combined with a more expressive or provocative content. As his work continues to develop in tune with current directions, he should not simply be seen in his historical role.

Peter Kubelka: *Adebar*, 1957

96

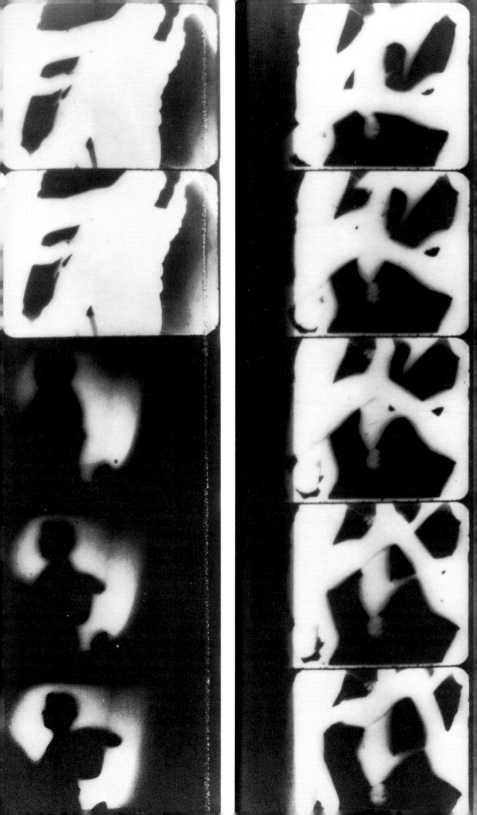

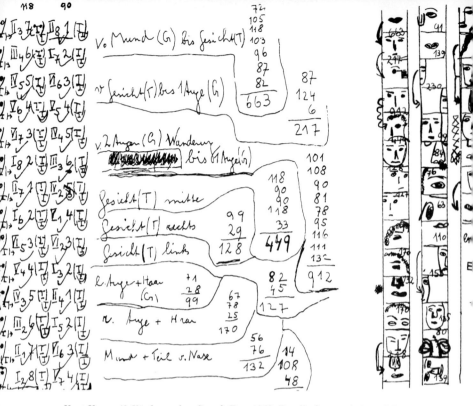

Kurt Kren: *48 Köpfe aus dem Szondi-Test*, 1960. Detail of systemic 'score' for the film
*right* Sequence from the film

There are two factors in the work of Kren which are of importance in the present context. First is a comparatively simple one, his initiation and consistent use of systemic structures; and second, a more complex set of questions concerning the relationship between structure, image and existential attitude. Possibly because his best known films are those which were made with Brus or Muehl, exponents of the Direct Art movement, he is often wrongly assumed to be primarily a documenter of that work. It is little realized that even these films were either shot or subsequently edited to mathematical structures.

Following early experiments on 8mm between 1953 and 1957, he made his first 16mm film *Versuch mit synthetischen Ton* (1957), including a drawn soundtrack beginning to develop the notions of formal relationships between simple images. But his next three films, made between then and 1961, showed the systemic direction of his work most clearly: *48 Köpfe aus dem Szondi-Test* (1960) and *Bäume im Herbst* (1960) being shot according to system, and *Mauern-Positiv-Negativ und Weg* (1961) being edited that way. It is also evident in these films and is confirmed in his next, *Fenstergucker, Abfall etc.* (1962), that even if Kren rejected poetic or narrative intention, the images of his work were in no way neutral, arbitrary or convenient fillers for a mathematical system.

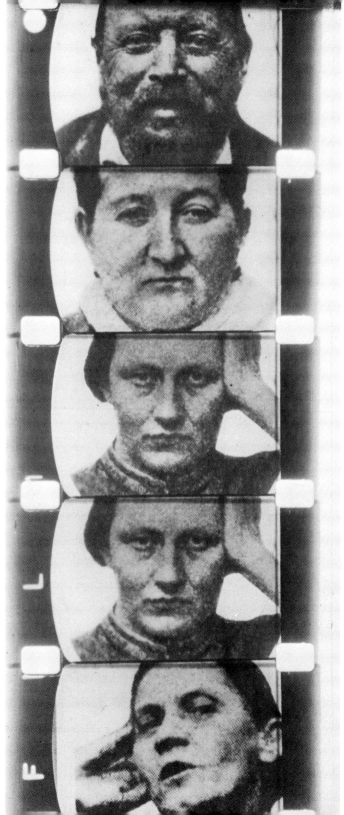

Kren, like Brakhage, must be seen in his relationship to existentialism. Certainly with Kren there is no autobiographical intention, but like Brakhage, his images derive essentially from his passage through the world as an individual, so that for both, the chief protagonist of the films is the person behind the camera. In the extreme of existentialism, choice is a result of immediate subjective response. Speaking of the French existentialists, including himself, Jean-Paul Sartre said: 'What they have in common is simply the fact that they believe that existence comes before essence—or, if you will, that we must begin from the subjective.'[3] This existentialist intention is central to the underground film. When film-makers like Godard, who derive from the commercial, narrative cinema, portray existentialism, their cinematic form is not existentialist, because it lacks the crucial 'first person' viewpoint. It is only in the underground film that this form has been developed, albeit slowly, against the background of cinematic conventions which have contrary purpose.

In the context of an existentialist attitude to cinema, and in the work of Kurt Kren, a new issue emerges. This can be seen as a dialectic between existentialism and structuralism, centring on the relationship between concept or pre-concept and subjective experience. In rejecting essence, and with it philosophical hierarchy and transcendence, existentialism is suspicious of all forms of structure on the grounds that they prevent immediate experiential relationship. Alternatively it sees structural order as authoritarian, a reflection of the dominance of the current social and environmental condition. This can also extend to a suspicion even of psycho-analytical order. However, there need be no fundamental conflict with order or structure, merely with the concept of order as an immutable condition—either existing *a priori* within phenomena, or as an accepted authoritarian determinant of choice. Particularly in art, order or, more precisely, ordering, becomes compatible with existentialism when that order is considered as temporary, local, provisional, fortuitous or arbitrary.

Perhaps the greatest conflict between existentialism and structuralism arises in the work of Lévi-Strauss, who is concerned with models to describe underlying 'deep structures' in dynamic social relationships. For dealing with complex phenomena, he maintains the classical concept of analytical reason, but with improved tools like transformational and matrix algebra. The conflict stems mainly from his maintenance of *a priori* assumptions about the structural relationships of phenomena.

On the other hand, some concepts expressed by Roland Barthes have the advantage of being more easily applicable to plastic art, and the virtue of showing a possible continuity between existential and structural art:

> The goal of all structuralist activity, whether reflexive or poetic, is to reconstruct an 'object' in such a way as to manifest thereby the rules of functioning (the 'functions') of this object. Structure is there for an actual simulacrum of the object, but a directed, interested simulacrum, since the imitated object makes something appear which remained invisible, or, if one prefers, unintelligible in the natural object.[4]

He then makes it clear that what results from this activity is something new, describing the resultant simulacrum as 'intellect added to object'.

Kurt Kren: *Bäume im Herbst*, 1960, showing hand-drawn soundtrack

This postulates the creative aspect of structure, for whilst it sees the structural activity taking place in relationship to the current state of phenomena, it sees the product as a specific new phenomenon. Compatibility between existentialism and structuralism therefore derives from the dialectical creation of structure for the perception and experience of existence. In effect, structuralism in art can be seen as a consequence of the awareness that concept can, and perhaps must, determine the nature of perception and experience if it is to avoid determination by existing convention and habit.

The first embodiment of this concept of structural activity in cinema comes in Kren's *Bäume im Herbst*, where the camera as subjective observer is constrained within a systemic or structural procedure, incidentally the precursor of the most structuralist aspect of Michael Snow's later work. In this film, perception of material relationships in the world is seen to be no more than a product of the structural activity in the work. Art forms experience. Barthes echoes this 'no more than' and says of it:

> Structural man takes the real, decomposes it, then recomposes it; this appears to be little enough (which makes some say the structuralist enterprise is 'meaningless', 'uninteresting', 'useless' etc.). Yet from another point of view, this 'little enough' is decisive: for between the two objects, or two tenses, of structuralist activity there occurs something new and what is new is no less than the generally intelligible.[5]

Though some subsequent works by Kren can be considered in directly similar terms, like *Grun Rot* (1968) and a film portrait of Peter Kochenrath (1973), and while certain aspects of his other systemic work may function similarly, other aspects of it are not easily relatable to structuralism. Structuralism in cinema is certainly not to be defined simply as the application of system to experience. As we get closer to contemporary work, there are formal developments which it would certainly be misleading to overanalyse in structural terms. I have already pointed out that Kren's images are in no way 'detached'—the image is not only a point of contact with the phenomenal world, but with Kren's particular experience of it. Another consequence of his subjective existentialism is an unwillingness to engage in large-scale, long-term works so that all his films have been short and succinct, dealing only with a range within which he can achieve an internal precision.

Although an approach to the imagist aspect of Kren's work is out of the scope of this book, we must look at some of the other contributions he has made to new formal developments. The systems of his early films were largely built on interchanging shots of relatively short duration, frequently a range of from one to twenty-four frames, that is, various fractions of a second. Sometimes the changes are linear and, even more frequently, they involve acceleration or deceleration of the rate of change, creating waves of interaction between shots. In *Mauern-Positiv-Negativ und Weg*, Kren introduced the interchange of negative and positive versions of the same image. As in Brakhage's *XV Song Traits, Michael McClure* (1965) in which he superimposes the negative and positive of the same image, the introduction of the negative in *Mauern* is not a graphic device for the transformation of image into abstract shape as it is in Kubelka's *Adebar* or in Richter's *Film Study*. Instead it opens up the possibility of seeing negative image as an element of the material process of cinema.

Following these two films and *Bäume im Herbst*, Kren's next important systemic film is *TV* (1967). In *TV*, the system is different in kind and pace to that which exists in much of his other work. Instead of operating primarily at the kinetic level, or with rapid perceptual rhythm, this film involves the audience in a conceptual and reflexive process. Five short sequences each about eight frames long ($\frac{1}{3}$ second) are all shot from the same viewpoint in a quay-side café. They show a window, broken by the silhouettes of objects and people within the café and by the passage of people and a ship outside. Each shot containing some small movement is repeated in the film twenty-one times, in mathematically determined order. They are separated by short, equal sequences of black spacing, except that longer black sequences separate

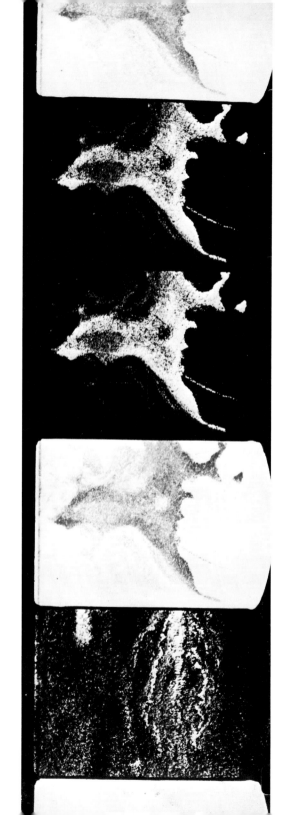

Kurt Kren:
*Mauern-Positiv-
Negativ und Weg,*
1961

larger phrases of repeats from each other rather like punctuation. Sometimes the same shots follow each other, sometimes all five shots occur in one phrase. The significance does not lie in the mathematical sequence as such, but in how the viewer attempts to decipher the structure. This overtly reflexive attitude to structure became important in a number of European films about this time (notably by Hein, Nekes, Gidal and myself), often incorporating image repetition. But none as clearly shifts the structural activity away from the interior construction of the film towards the deliberate exterior reflexiveness of the audience as does *TV* (incidentally prefiguring Frampton's *Zorns Lemma* of 1971). An additional value which *TV* has as a film (over *Zorns Lemma*) is the depth of its control of image and motion at levels other than the systemic. The qualities of motion within the shots, and their pace, relate directly to the duration of the shots and the duration of the spaces between. The nature of the similarities between the images and motion is such that the reflexive mode of the viewer is taken through a number of distinguishable phases, as first the images themselves are recognized and defined, then remembered, then their sequence noted and compared via memory. The reflexive activity constantly interacts with the kinetic and associative aspect of the images and their distribution.

The next year, in 1968, Kren made *Venecia kaputt*, which lasts only six seconds, and utilizes scratching on film to erase an image of Venice. And in the same year he made *Schatzi*, which explored the irony of a formal image device, the interplay of negative and positive superimposition, involving the viewer in the material interaction only to reveal finally that the picture is of an army officer surveying a field of corpses. In many respects, Kren's work continues to express the tension between the existential and the structural. His formal inclinations and systemic structures never become formalist or a formula unrelated to the existential aspect of image.

Before passing on to the mass of work in formal cinema which has been completed since 1966, I should point out that Marc Adrian was an important contributor to the situation in which Kren and Kubelka worked, though his films, particularly his early experiments with an improvised form of computer-generated film in *Random* (1963), *Text I* and *Text II* (both 1964), rarely seem fully realized works.

# 9 · Around 1966

Between 1966 and the present time, the formal aspect of avant-garde film has exploded to become its mainstream. The period since the beginning of 1966 can be split roughly into two. Up to about the end of 1968 many of the directions which have been explored since were opened up by a number of film-makers, now considered as a 'first generation' of the new formal movement. Since 1968 there has been a further clarification and consolidation of some directions, the emergence from them of new problems, and a large 'second generation' of film-makers.

It must be pointed out that most existing literature about the development of this aspect of cinema has a very misleading bias. Originating, as most of it does, in American books and magazines, written by American critics who have developed their critical approach from experience of the underground film in America, reference to European work in this field has been confined almost entirely to that of Peter Kubelka so that it would appear from all the best-known writing that this direction of cinema was almost exclusively an American phenomenon. This is quite inaccurate. In the first generation of the new formal work five of the significant film-makers are American—George Landow, Tony Conrad, Ken Jacobs, Paul Sharits and Peter Gidal (all of whose work has been made in London); two are Canadian—Michael Snow and Joyce Wieland; whilst at least ten are from Europe—Kurt Kren, Peter Kubelka, Peter Weibel, Valie Export and Ernst Schmidt Jnr (Austrian), Birgit and Wilhelm Hein, Werner Nekes and Lutz Mommartz (German), and myself (British). In the period following 1968 the predominance of developments in formal cinema swings if anything even more strongly towards European work.

Because the numbers involved are so large, I shall trace the development of broad areas of inquiry to which the film-makers have contributed, instead of tracing the work of individual film-makers. Many of the film-makers, especially the first generation, have contributed to a wide range of developments, sometimes within single films. Work of the individuals is in most cases worthy of more attention than it can receive here: a much fuller account is needed to do justice to the last ten years, now that its historical context begins to be clearer.

The first area of inquiry to look at is the perceptual film. The term normally used for it is the 'flicker film', though it is too specific to define it by a single characteristic rather than its region of function. This area of cinema attempts to examine, or create experience through devices which work on the autonomic nervous system. Where the main characteristic of Op Art in painting is the use of simultaneous contrasts in sufficiently close planar relationship to stimulate an essentially retinal reaction, in film this reaches its purest form in a concentration on the temporal equivalent—rapid sequential contrasts. Duchamp's *Anemic Cinéma*, at least in relationship to the revolving visual discs, directly initiates perceptual cinema. Other work in the abstract field has also tended towards an optical phase, where the kinetic aspects of interior motion are replaced by large-scale change of whole areas of the screen. Editing of live-action sequences in the avant-garde film has increasingly tended towards extremely rapid rates of change. One possible motive for this is an implicit search for a film which can function essentially on the psycho-physical rather than the psycho-interpretative level. Action on the autonomic system seeks to create a nervous response which is largely pre-conscious, the psychological reactions sought being a direct consequence of physiological function.

Cinema, as a mechanism, is designed to project one separate picture every 1/24 second. If the period during which the projection shutter is closed is taken into account, each image occupies the screen for approximately half that time, about 1/50 second, while the rate of image change in film is deliberately located just beyond the point where the eye can discern flicker. This factor is economic using the smallest number of separate images necessary to create smooth movement. However, film's 'location' on this optical threshold makes it ideally suitable for examining the threshold itself by exposure to optical events and rates of change which move progressively into the region where flicker is discerned, by increasing the ratio of dark to light frames in increments of 1/24 second.

The first film to show this perceptual possibility in an extreme form is Kubelka's *Arnulf Rainer*. However much its retinal bombardment of alternating short black and white sequences may initiate optical effects, like that of colour after-image, the film is constructed in such a way that no stroboscopic rates are maintained in a sufficiently unbroken sequence to allow it to be described as concerned with the optical factors. The first such film is Tony Conrad's *The Flicker*, made six years later, in 1966, and conceived entirely in terms of retinal response. It explores different stroboscopic systems first, and then systematic interactions between them. The result is a film which enables awareness of changing modes of response to recognizably different strobe conditions—awareness of how the autonomic response begins to shade off into pattern recognition as the black and white units increase in length; how the different systems interact; how the difference in colour after-image relates to different strobe rates; and possibly becoming aware of other physiological changes as the retinal activity affects the rhythm of other areas of the nervous system.

In the same year, Paul Sharits made *Ray Gun Virus*, a fourteen-minute film with no images, which explores the optical interaction of single-colour frames. Also in 1966 he completed two other films which rely heavily on the optical interaction of colour, but both of these, *Word Movie* and *Piece Mandala (End War)* also contain associative material, in the first instance rapidly changing words, in the second single-frame images of himself and a couple. It is only in *Ray Gun Virus* and *N:o:t:h:i:n:g;* (1968) that the optical experience is uninterrupted by associative or semantic issues which also encroach on his longer optical colour works of 1968, *Razor Blades* and *T,O,U,C,H,I,N,G*.

In his work as a whole we see a pull in three directions. The first is the obvious factor of colour interactions in time, which affect the retina; the second is a confusing romanticism which results in unintegrated images and inappropriate interpretation of the material aspect of the experience; the third is a systemic intention in the overall form of his films. The interesting interaction is between the first and last. It is in the nature of

Tony Conrad: *The Flicker*, 1966

the autonomic experience that it should be localized in the immediate clusters of perception, counteracting awareness of his overall systemic concept. Whilst in Conrad's *The Flicker* the overall experience is due to awareness of gradually changing modes of perception, with Sharits the structural concepts are conceived in terms of two-dimensional pattern through which the film traces a particular path. It is perhaps his awareness of the difficulty of perceiving the formal pattern during the projection of his films that has recently led him to explore an alternative presentation of some as a matrix—whole films installed as adjacent strips between plexi-glass, where the system becomes immediately apparent. In his optical colour work, even after seeing the system in this static way, I have found it impossible to experience it from the sequential presentation of the films.

Other film-makers have produced works which directly explore one or another aspect of the perceptual film, mostly involving the extreme of white and black interchange, though some developments have also been made in the area of colour. Since 1966, the perceptual problem in cinema has become a fairly clear area of study. There are two works which have sought to increase the contrast between black and white by using the extremely light-resistant magnetic sound recording stock, out of which holes of a single-frame duration are punched. In America Taka Iimura presented some loop projection experiments using this technique in 1969, and my own film *Spot the Microdot* using the same technique was made independently in 1970.

Birgit and Wilhelm Hein began a number of consistent studies in the perceptual area with *625* (1969), the strobe being achieved by refilming at different camera speeds from an imageless television screen. They followed this in the same year by an untitled film (part 3 of *Work in Progress* reel A), in which a single still image was interchanged with black film spacing, three frames of each at a time, for approximately ten minutes. In this work, the Heins uncovered a curious visual phenomenon. Not only can continuous strobe produce colour as after-image, but it can also create an illusion of motion where none exists. The still picture of two girls seated together, continuously repeated, gradually seems to move, the faces seem to smile, and one figure seems to lean closer to the other. The cause of this phenomenon may be similar to the inevitable mental re-ordering of repeated verbal phrases. The perceptual process seems to demand change even where there is none. In the near scientific way in which they have come increasingly to follow up their experiments, the Heins made *Foto-Film* (1970) which further tested this phenomenon. Like Iimura and myself, using the light-resistant magnetic stock for maximum contrast, they produced a flicker film which could be projected over a large still photograph attached to the screen. The effect of apparent motion remained, even though in this case it could not be explained by possible small movements (jittering) in the projected picture.

Their most developed work in this field is not stroboscopic. Made in four parts during 1971–2, it is a two-screen film titled *Doppelprojection I–IV*. Various rates of rapid fade are explored, with a completely blank screen in two of the parts, and with a simple static camera shot (not a refilmed still) in the other two parts. The optical response in this film is directly related to the two-screen format, where the fading screen shifts the eye continuously backwards and forwards from one to the other, sometimes causing an apparent lateral rotation of the screen surface. Like many works in this area, and particularly in the Heins' perceptual work, the screen itself and its illumination become extremely physical.

As in the Op Art of Victor Vasarely and Josef Albers, or the spirals of Duchamp, the illusion factor is significantly different when it is the result of physical experience, than when it is the illusionism of spurious pictorial or narrative involvement. It is an area in which we may genuinely study ourselves and our reactions. Conrad explored the possibilities of this form with *Straight and Narrow* (1970), and the four-screen film *Four Square* (1971), which includes exploration of colour interchange. Also in 1971 the British film-maker Fred Drummond made *Green Cut Gate*, a two-screen colour film based largely on a regular perceptual flicker.

The next general area of exploration is the loop and image repetition. Though the history of the loop as a formal device in film began with Léger's woman climbing the stairs in *Ballet Mécanique*, Thomas Edison first solved his film presentation problem in 1889 by the Kinetoscope, a loop-film viewing-machine, and the earlier precursors of cinema, the Zoetropes, were in effect small, closed loop experiences. Exactly when the possibility of image repetition was first taken up as the major basis of a film's form is difficult to decide. There are at least three inter-connected issues: loops in the projector; printing loops onto continuous film as a more permanent replacement for projection loops or as a basis for developing transformational repetition; the repetition of film sequences without the rhythmic aspect of loop structure.

In the first case, projection loops are by their nature transient, as they wear out rapidly, and work in this area is often undocumented. George Landow, certainly one of the first film-makers to explore the projection of loops, records that his *Film in which there appear Sprocket Holes, Edge Lettering, Dirt Particles etc.* (1966) began its life as a projected loop. Many of my own earliest film experiments were of this kind, and I

George Landow: *Film in which there appear Sprocket Holes,*
*Edge Lettering, Dirt Particles etc.*, 1966

suspect that other film-makers who began experimenting in the mid-sixties followed similar paths. Most of what now survives is the result of having the loops printed onto continuous film, as Landow did.

Landow pursued the idea of repetition in his next film, *Bardo Follies* (1967), where the loop begins to be a much more complex device. A loop of a woman waving to a passing riverboat is later optically printed, so that, for example, three images of the same loop occupy different sections of the screen. A complex rhythm is established by the loops beginning at different points in the action. The major section of the film involves the continuous repetition of an image, what seems to be a burning or blistering film frame, which may either be loop-printed, or the result of a repeated action.

Bruce Connor, in *Report* (1965), incorporated the repetition of the passing of John F. Kennedy's car at the moment of his assassination. In this film, the repetition is included within the film as an expressive device and as a 'study replay' of the transient event, a technique with which we have since become familiar in the 'action replay' of television. However, Connor's use of the device is not part of the development of loop or repetition as a central basis of form.

The issue of repetition, partial repetition and transforming repetition has been a significant feature of much of my own work, particularly of my earliest films between 1966 and 1968. Using the loop in the rhythmic sense, rather than for systematic or edited repetition, is most developed in *Yes No Maybe Maybenot* and *Little Dog for Roger* (both 1967). In my case, using the loop has been related to transformation in printing. Both these films have a similar complexity of rhythmic experience to that which is found in *Bardo Follies*. But by changing the lengths of the loop, and by superimposing and interchanging loops of different lengths, more complex rhythmic phases are explored. In *Yes No Maybe Maybenot* the interior kinetic of waves breaking against a barrier, or smoke coming from a chimney, combines with the inherent rhythmic phase created by the loop repetition.

Two other films of 1967 contribute significantly to this direction. In both *Sailboat* by Joyce Wieland and *Gertrug 1* by Werner Nekes, though exact repetition is uncertain, the idea of loop repetition is established as the underlying structural reference. This is broken down by uncompleted repetition or sequences which may be film of repeated action rather than loop-reprintings. This is similar to the function of repetition in Kren's film *TV*.

Without the kinetic element of repeated loops, repetition of identifiable elements is an essential prerequisite for the establishment of systemic structure. My own films, *Castle 1* (1966) and the quite separate two-screen *Castle 2* (1968), both make use of multiple repeats of a small number of basic sequences. Though both films use 'found' newsreel-type footage, the primary structural experience is based on establishing and tracing various alternative editing patterns. A similar structural re-organization of repeated images is also one possible understanding of three films from around this time based on still photographs: Kren's *48 Köpfe aus dem Szondi-Test* (1962) (see illustrations pages 98–99) is a systemic sequential organization of a set of photographs originally intended for an obscure psychological test; Drummond's *Photo-film based on Muybridge* (1968) and another untitled section of *Work in*

Birgit and Wilhelm
Hein: *Work in
Progress* (part 6,
reel A, 1969)

Peter Gidal: *Hall*, 1968

*Progress* (part 6, reel A, 1969) by the Heins, are based on the synthesis of previously analysed action.

In Kren's film the original photographs were in no way conceived in terms of motion. However, his system, by exploring various visual relationships between the pictures, in some instances creates apparent animation between the unrelated pictures. Animated motion is not the only result of his system, it is only one form of the various kinds of visual interaction between nearly similar elements. Sometimes the editing rhythm is the dominant experience, sometimes in close-up the half-screen dots of the images interact in a textural swirl.

Drummond's film, as the title suggests, is based mainly on the motion analysis photographs of Eadweard Muybridge, though their reconstruction and synthesis do not always follow the original chronology, but create new patterns of relationship. As a 'structural' possibility this is really taken up as the main intention of the later Hein film. A very short sequence of a figure running across a room was shot, from which still photographs were made at intervals, and the final film shot from various re-combinations and re-orderings of this fragmented action (page 111).

Of the three films which explore this possibility, the Heins' film has given clearest focus on the frame-by-frame nature of cinematography, and the question of motion analysis/synthesis. It refutes Bragaglia's claim that 'cinematography never analyses movement' but shatters it in the film-strip and 'merely reconstructs fragments of reality' instead of synthesizing them.[1] By re-analysing and re-ordering the images from the original film-strip, their film not only constitutes synthesis, but creative synthesis in the sense of providing a new phenomenon, revealing the capabilities of cinematography as a way of forming experience of the world.

Another work from this period, *Room, Double Take* (1967) by Peter Gidal, and three of his later films, *Hall* (1968), *Loop* (1968) and *Clouds* (1969), make important contributions to the function of image repetition. In *Room, Double Take* and *Hall*, he makes deliberate use of the device of the complete repetition of a whole film. In the first, a five-minute pan around a room ends on a man smoking. The camera's movement is slow and in close-up on the objects it passes, causing the viewer to mentally search ahead of its motion particularly in the repeat. In *Hall*, systematic editing from long, mid and close shots of a hall and its objects again encourages the viewer to predict what will be shown. The complete repetition in both these films is a device for a second 'look' at material which has already been the subject of a predictive, reflexive process, this time through memory with a view slightly ahead of the next development. In *Clouds*, the passage of an aeroplane just visible in an indistinct sky is repeated, sometimes in the negative, so that, as in Wieland's *Sailboat*, it is never certain if the repeat is the result of re-printing or the passage of another plane.

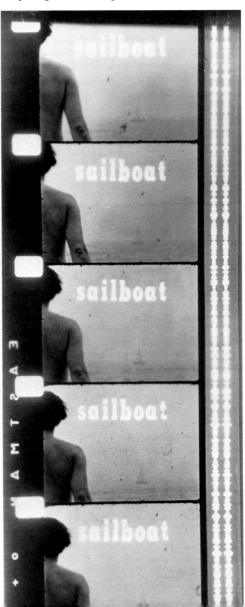

Joyce Wieland:
*Sailboat*, 1967

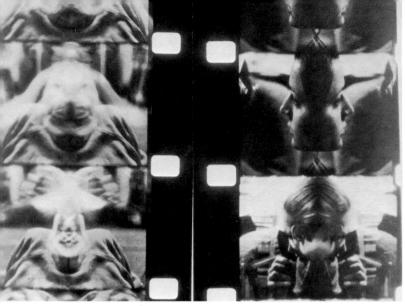

Hollis Frampton: *Artificial Light*, 1969

implications of changing forms of visual/kinetic information—an awareness of transforming experience. Except for *Yes No Maybe Maybenot*, most of the formative work in transformation through printing took place in 1969. A little-known contributor to this development in cinema is the Swiss Klaus Schönherr, who, unaware of my own work, reacted to the lack of control and understanding of the printing process by constructing his own equipment. His first work to exploit the potential of changing image quality through this stage also came in 1969: *Play 4 and 5*. In the same year Hollis Frampton made *Artificial Light*, which, though it is not solely concerned with plastic transformation through printing, uses it as one strategy in twenty transformational variations on a basic sequence of film.

A technique which has led film-makers into similar areas as those concerned with the transformation through printing, is the refilming of material from the screen. This has much in common with the more sophisticated methods of optical printing which allow images to be frozen, run in reverse, sections of the picture to be reframed or blown-up, but because of the simplicity of setting up a camera in front of a screen, it has a greater flexibility and is much more available than most optical printing facilities. If Ken Jacobs' much discussed *Tom Tom the Piper's Son* (1969) provides the most extensive exploration of this technique, basing the whole ninety-minute film on the abstract transformation of a short sequence of early movie, the Heins, with *Grün* and *Roh Film* ('raw film') (both 1968) must take the credit for first grasping the potential of this method.

In *Grün*, a sequence of 'holiday' film is examined minutely from the screen of an editing machine, making use of all the possibilities of stopping the image, pulling frames through by hand, revealing the frame structure and so on. Though both the Heins' and Jacobs' films show a 'self-awareness' of the process and the medium as material, neither takes on the problem of the act of refilming as subject, as do some more

116

recent works. Instead they utilize the technique either towards an expressive end, as in *Grün*, or towards the visual abstraction of the image as in *Tom Tom*. Refilming in *Roh Film* is of a different kind, and this film plays a major part in the next area of inquiry fundamental to the recent history of avant-garde film.

One general understanding of all the film tendencies under discussion could be in terms of their shift towards the establishment of film as 'material' (this would stand up at least as well, if not better than, the 'structural' generalization). Whatever its value as a generalization, at the present I am using it much more specifically to refer to the use and examination of the physical aspects of the film material as a basis of film image and structure. Three key works, produced quite independently of each other between 1966 and 1968, are similar to a remarkable degree in their deliberate attention to the film material itself as the basis of image. All three concentrated on a number of film's quite basic factors, which had to that point largely been ignored as incidental supports for what was assumed to be the 'real' subject matter of cinema. The three films are: *Film in which there appear Sprocket Holes, Edge Lettering, Dirt*

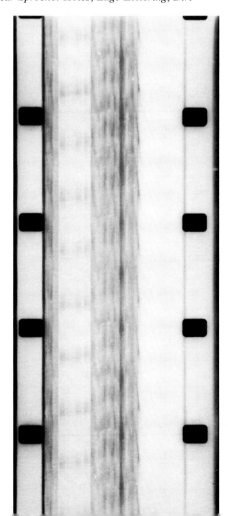

Malcolm Le Grice:
*Little Dog for
Roger*, 1967–8

*Particles etc.* (1966) by Landow, my own *Little Dog for Roger* (1967 and double-projection version, 1968) and the Heins' *Roh Film.* Of course, all three films have quite different 'characters' even though each incorporates all the elements blandly listed in the title of the Landow film, and the latter two films add to its 'etc.': celluloid scratches, processing stains, splicing-tape marks, finger-prints, and image slip (see illustration page 117). Not only are the films concerned to include cinematic elements basic to it as a mechanism, like the sprocket-holes, the celluloid support, and the emulsion as material, but also to include elements which are usually considered as error, fault or in cybernetic terms, noise. This is particularly true of *Little Dog for Roger* and *Roh Film* which, as well as referring to the physical aspects of the film strip, also refer to material aspects like the act of splicing and to the functioning of the projector. For example, in *Little Dog for Roger* there is a long section of image slip, where the material is disengaged from the printer claw, deliberately simulating the skidding of film in the projector.

The main difference between Landow's film and that of the Heins and myself, is that his is essentially a semantic or semiotic work: the visual elements refer to the material aspects of film in much the same way that a sign refers to an object. The two films made in Europe, how-ever, create much of their experience through evident tactility and evident process: traces of the films' handling are deliberately retained. They attack the implicit alienation in the film process which loses contact with the vital stages of image transfer and chemical development, and both are the result of contact between the film-maker and film at all stages.

The Heins mostly achieved their images by putting many kinds of material through a projector, often consisting of three or four film-strips physically collaged and refilmed from the screen. In *Little Dog for Roger*, much of the material was produced on a primitive printer converted from a projector, and long sections were produced by direct contact printing of an original 9·5mm home movie onto 16mm in short strips under glass. Sometimes the resultant 16mm strips were similarly treated in a second generation, creating an image of film-strip on film-strip—the film edges and sprockets of both generations interacting. All three films, but particularly the last two, should be considered as clarify-ing the direction begun by Man Ray in *Retour à la Raison*, continued in Lye's *Colour Box* (1935) and Brakhage's *Mothlight*, and, as a latent aspect, in the whole tradition of the hand-made film. Later work by Landow like *Remedial Reading Comprehension* (1970) has confirmed that his involvement is more fundamentally semiotic than with the film as physical experience. On the other hand, later work by the Heins and myself has continued to explore film or cinema as material phenomena and processes.

In 1967, the issue of duration began to emerge as central in a number of films by different film-makers, again quite independently but with great divergence in their particular direction: *Und Sie?* by the Heins, *Eisen-bahn* by Mommartz, *Room, Double Take* by Gidal, *Wavelength* by Snow and my own *Blind White Duration*. In one way or another, all five films establish experience of duration as a 'concrete' dimension of cinema, and

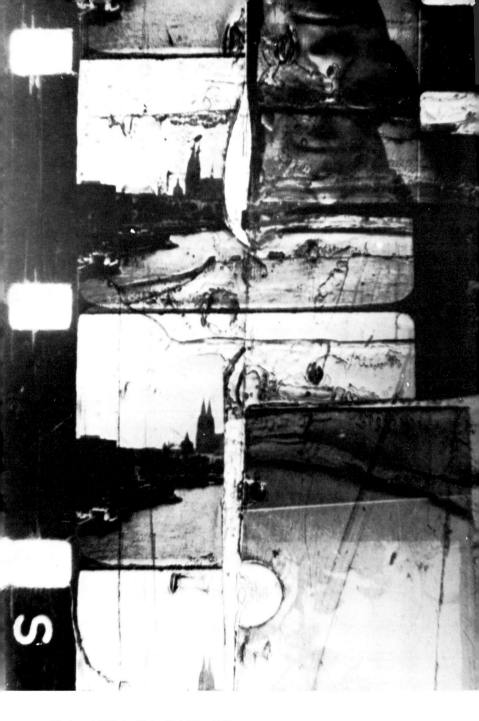

Birgit and Wilhelm Hein: *Roh Film*, 1968

as the dominant dimension of cinematic experience. *Wavelength*'s forty-five-minute zoom through a room and into a still photograph on the wall is seen both as an extension from Warhol's static camera, and the basis of the film's shape. However, its main confusion comes through a premature compromise between durational continuity in the Warhol manner, and illusory narrative time of a different order. Whilst a surface continuity is achieved for the projection duration through the apparent consistency of the zoom and the rising sine-wave sound, this is no more than a co-ordinating device for its illusory interior duration. One-to-one relationship between the projection duration and the shooting duration is lost through breaks in the shooting not made clear in the form of the film. By utilizing a contrived continuity to parallel the implied time of its narrative, the film is in some ways a retrograde step in cinematic form. Its real context is narrative cinema, and as such it may open other important questions. In *Wavelength*, as in certain aspects of ←→, this narrative virtuosity confuses the advance of a material concept of cinema, but which other aspects of these films and other of his works, notably *The Central Region*, advance significantly.

The durational issue is most clearly dealt with by Snow in two films from 1969, *Dripping Water* (made with Wieland), and *One Second in Montreal*. My own *Blind White Duration* (1967) has some features in common with this film; for example, the images in both cases are of city streets under snow. However, though there was no narrative intention of any kind in *Blind White Duration*, the film can be criticized similarly to *Wavelength*, in that it does establish an 'implied' duration of quite a different order to the material duration of the film. *Wavelength* incorporates three daylight periods, separated by darkness outside the window, an implicit span of three days; *Blind White Duration* incorporates material shot in one day and a night, returning to the same morning material after the night within the film, an implied duration of just over a day-and-night cycle within the film's twelve minutes. The main aim in *Blind White Duration*, which is achieved much more clearly in my recent film *White Field Duration* (1973), is to establish the length of projection time as a material experience by exposing the viewer to a white screen. In *Blind White Duration* this aim is counteracted somewhat by the incorporation of material which refers to a time and space not concretely present in the projection event.

*One Second in Montreal* also attempts to establish a concrete duration, which it does by exposing the viewer to a series of unexceptional still images. As each still is shown for much longer than it took to expose in the camera, the viewing time is an extreme extension of the 'shooting' time. The succession of pictures follow a recognizable pattern of increasing, then decreasing periods of presentation, thus allowing qualitative awareness of the relationship of durational experience to the rate of change of presented information. In the first part of the film the duration of each still increases progressively causing the inevitable withdrawal of involvement by the spectator—boredom. Curiously, however, in the second period of the film where the durations decrease, the eye, trained by the search in the earlier period, is frustrated by the removal of an image where it had previously been frustrated by its prolongation.

In the Heins' *Und Sie?*, one single image is maintained for the eleven minutes of the film, only being changed through minimal shifts in focus, the image being mostly in soft focus throughout. The technique of continual exposure to a still image is closely related to Warhol's use of the freeze frame in *Sleep*, and Snow's later use in *One Second in Montreal*. However, in the Heins' film attention is continually encouraged by minimal changes of the surface and focus of the image, and continually discouraged by inability to clearly identify the picture. Durational experience in this case is seen to be a function of perceptual attention.

Finally the other two films from 1967, *Eisenbahn* and *Room, Double Take*, deal with experience of duration in relationship to repetition. In Gidal's *Room (Double Take)*, as in his *Hall*, awareness of the film's length is changed considerably by the repeat. As in *One Second in Montreal*, 'perception training' in the first half of the film seems to diminish the duration of the second period.

In Mommartz's *Eisenbahn*, the continual view of a swiftly passing landscape, seen through the frame of a train window, poses the question of whether the image is the result of a loop, a long repetition, or is one continuous, unbroken take. Again absence of surprise or any extreme change of information gives a continuity to the experience of presentation time, not displaced by the viewer coming to discern a systematic pattern of relationships. Steve Dwoskin has also explored Warhol's idea of the continuous take in a number of films, particularly *Soliloquy* (1967). However, his work is never expressly concerned with formal aspects, but always retains a strong interior content and dramatic intention.

In effect, as with perceptual enquiry, the durational issue in film has become very much concerned with the viewer's changing state as content in itself, rather than with an interior content to which the viewer reacts. Since Warhol, film-makers have often used boredom as a cinematic principle. Many of the films discussed here discourage involvement in their action or system, so that the duration may be experienced as an actual event in the 'life' of the viewer. This invariably means eliminating frequent and obvious change, the normal source of 'information' in cinema. By reducing the information within the film to an extreme degree, the viewer's awareness of change shifts to his own changing response, and, in these films, particularly to the material passage of time.

Also consistent with the 'material' tendency of recent formal work is the direction which concentrates on the projector and projection. Unfortunately, like Sitney's 'structural film', Youngblood's term 'expanded cinema' has to be clarified before the term can be useful. Youngblood's book was published in 1970, but Peter Weibel in Austria had used the term about his own work as early as 1967. Wherever it originated, its connotations for Youngblood do not fit the extensive amount of European work being done in this area. Youngblood understands it mainly in terms of American West Coast abstraction, centring on film-makers like Jordan Belson and Scott Bartlett, and heavily linked to the idea of mind expansion, psychedelia and McLuhan's global village concept of televisual communication. In Europe, on the other hand, it is seen as a development of the formal issues of cinema and a concern with the reality of the projection situation itself. The only significant point of overlap is with new technology like the computer or video-synthesizer, though this is of diminishing concern in the European framework. A quite arbitrary point of contact is in the field of multi-projection: European aims have been almost exclusively formal, frequently conceptual and didactic, and have nothing in common with experiments in 'total' visual environments characterized by the work of Stan Vanderbeek in the mid-sixties.

The background for this development in Europe stems mostly from three sources: in Britain from my involvement with the projection situation as a material reality, and with comparative double projection; in Germany with a short foray into double projection by Werner Nekes and Lutz Mommartz for a similar purpose; and in Austria as a result of the Direct Art movement becoming increasingly concerned with formal, cinematic issues through the work of Peter Weibel and Valie Export. This 'formal' expanded cinema did not really begin until after 1968, and the most interesting examples exist in quite recent work representing a direction for which there is little equivalent in America.

The work between 1966 and 1968 which prefigures current developments does so at a rather primitive level. My first 16mm film *Castle 1* (1966) was designed for projection side by side with a bare electric lightbulb which flashed on and off, periodically illuminating the audience and the projection space, while at the same time washing out much of the image on the screen. Film of the same bulb was incorporated into long sequences of the film, connecting the interior aspect of the film with the transient conditions of the time and space in which it was projected.

Warhol's *Chelsea Girls* (1966) used double projection, two screens side by side, though the intention was quite different to that in Nekes' *Gurtrug Nr 2* (1967), my own *Yes No Maybe Maybenot* (1967), *Little Dog for Roger* (two-screen version 1968) and *Castle 2* (1968), and Mommartz's *Links/rechts* and *Gegenüber* (both 1968). For Warhol, double projection was partly a way of presenting the lengthy material in half its time but though it functioned like the simultaneous observation of two rooms, there is no deliberate formal interaction between the screens. In *Gurtrug Nr 2* and my own two-screen films, on the other hand, visual interaction between the screens is essential. Nekes makes a simple comparison between inverted images of the same material; *Yes No Maybe Maybenot* is a simple comparison between a negative and a positive print, from an already superimposed negative and positive image. In *Little Dog for Roger*, the two projectors run at different speeds, one at silent (sixteen frames per second), the other at sound speed (twenty-four frames per second) thus creating a gradual shift between the two screens. In *Castle 2*, the two screens follow different editing orders for the same sequences of film.

The two films by Mommartz (which I have never been able to see) by all accounts directly prefigure some of the more discursive uses which are currently being explored. Birgit Hein describes the films as follows:

In *Links/rechts* [Mommartz] relates the action of one screen to the other, as in a pillow-fight where the pillow is thrown from one screen to the other. In *Gegenüber*, both pictures and reality are present at the same time. A boy and a girl project onto each other. They each have a projector with film running through it, whilst an image of the same action is projected onto the screen behind them.[2]

Peter Weibel is perhaps the most didactic of the European film-makers, always relating his work directly to a theoretical position and of late often choosing to present it in the context of an explanatory lecture. His works frequently take on the nature of a demonstration of theoretical principles and have become increasingly rhetorical. After a short period of involvement with Otto Mühl and Gunther Brus, during 1967 and 1968, he and Export together presented a range of film and live-action works conceived in terms of a deliberate challenge to the limits of cinema.

Weibel's work of this period is often transient or provocative, like *Exit* (1968) where he obscures the film running on the cinema screen by a portable screen erected in front of it, lights fireworks in the audience and leaves. His work has always been concerned with the structure of information, and its relationship to the whole continuum of electro-magnetic radiation. His concept of expanded cinema is directly related to his awareness of the narrow band of 'informational radiation' used in normal cinema. He has, therefore, been concerned with technology in the sense of attempting to extend cinema into the full electromagnetic range, and in showing the nature of informational relationships.

In *Das magische Auge* ('the magic eye', 1969) a film is projected on to a screen wired up with light sensors and the signals received from these in response to the changing pattern of light on the screen are then transformed into simple sound patterns. His intention is not simply to create sound from light, but to demonstrate how information can be divorced from specific semantic implications and instead seen as a physical, material problem. In this respect, all his provocation is directed towards a questioning of the nature of information, the most aggressive works demonstrating the relationship between information and authority.

Valie Export's work from this period, on the other hand, is more contained and durable. This is seen in film and action pieces like *Ping Pong* (1968) where a table is set up touching the base of the screen and a film is projected of herself sending balls outwards. At the same time, she hits a real ball backwards and forwards against the screen with as much success as possible. In *Cutting* (1968), she uses scissors to cut the words of a message 'the content of the writing is . . . ' from a screen illuminated by the light of an empty projector, whilst in another piece she attempts to draw on the screen the outline of a projected statue, as it jitters from the movement of a hand-held camera. All her film work is short, succinct and directly related to a single concept.

Ernst Schmidt Jnr makes his most interesting contribution to this aspect of cinema in *Ja/Nein* (1968), where film of the curtains of a cinema being drawn backwards and forwards is projected whilst the actual curtains of the cinema are similarly moved. A little later, in 1969, the Swiss Dieter Meier produced a number of blandly conceptual works, the best of which were four self-portraits, *Selbstportrait A, B, C* and *D* in which he stood before the screen for one minute followed by a one-minute film taken of him on the previous day, the dates and projection times being recorded.

# 10 · Current developments

The period since 1969 has seen a great proliferation of work in the formal direction of cinema. At this stage it becomes increasingly difficult to maintain a satisfactory chronology and classification. I generalize with reservation, mostly as a guide to a film's 'purpose' and a provisional ordering of the field as a whole. More than at any other time, film-makers are being influenced by seeing each other's work and reacting to it very soon after its making. Most of the film-makers have an awareness of the whole range of current developments, although this is less true of the American film-makers who see little of the European work. For the first time, the avant-garde film can be seen as an international movement with a real cultural impetus, the individual film-makers no longer working in isolation. Film-makers now confront the problem of 'the next step' informed of the historical situation and in the context of a contribution to issues which are cultural rather than primitively idio-syncratic. The main function of my schema for recent developments is to allow a scan of the film-makers and some of their work. Although it may provide a useful basis for analysis, there is not yet sufficient historical distance for confident assessment.

I shall begin by considering films where the event on the screen is essentially to be considered as the direct record of an event which took place in and through the camera, that is, films which largely do not involve any later transformation through editing or reprocessing. However, they may be related to some kind of systemic or procedural condition at the time of shooting, and they all assume that the camera cannot be ignored as neutral—they are films which in some way or other extend the deliberate, strategic aspect of camera function. Historically, they can be seen as an extension from Brakhage's subjective camera of the late fifties, its systemic use in Kren's *Bäume im Herbst* (1960) and Warhol's single-take films of 1963 and 1964. This area could be broadly split in two, even though there are considerable overlaps; on the one hand essentially systemic work, following a fixed strategy, and on the other, procedural work, seeking to control the situation and the broad issues of approach whilst responding to the immediate act of realization.

Some of the current systemic uses of the camera have developed from involvement in a strict time-lapse form conceived in terms of a controlled observational device. Interesting work in this area has been done by William Raban and Chris Wellsby, both separately and, earlier, in collaboration. Their most important work together is *River Yar* (1971) which comprises a three-week period in autumn and a three-week period in spring, time-lapsed day and night. Each three-week period is taken from an identical viewpoint, overlooking a river, and is recorded on thirty-five minutes of film, the spring and autumn sequences being projected side by side in a two-screen format.

Since this film, both have explored different systemic structures for the camera, sometimes a strict sampling of time-based units, sometimes using other determinants for the length of a sample. For example, in Raban's *Basement Window* (1970) a sequence is taken whenever someone passes outside the window. In Wellsby's *Windmill II* (1971) the camera motor speed is mechanically determined by the rate at which a windmill turns—as the wind speed increases, so does the camera speed, causing the visible effects of the wind in the trees to retain a constant textural movement, whilst other events, like traffic movement and film exposure, vary in response to the changes. In his *Running Film* (1972), each shot lasts for ten seconds while a figure runs away from the camera as far as he can in the time, returning and repeating the action for each ten-second burst. Time determines a body/action space. Another of his works exploring wind speed and direction as a determinant of the observational sample is his most 'organic' film, the two-screen *Wind Vane Film* (versions made in 1970 and 1972). In this, two cameras were mounted side by side on tripods where the panning heads were attached to wind-vanes. The cameras and a stereo tape-recorder were then set running and the camera direction and movement determined by the wind.

Raban has not followed the systemic observational direction as exclusively as has Wellsby, having also produced work in quite different directions, but the films which he has made in this field have either tended towards a concern with the factor of exposure time, or have sought a human, bodily determinant for the time or space sampling. Unlike Wellsby, Raban is concerned with the problem of real-time equivalence in the Warhol sense, and has always shown a need to context the compression of time with the actual shooting duration, sometimes including sequences of normal-time shooting as a reference. More recently he has made a number of films which are made in short takes but are edited to include the time between takes as recorded by continuously running sound.

He began to develop this form in *Soft Edge* (1973) where the take length is determined by the wind-down of the clockwork motor of the camera, and the intervening period of rewinding is black; the two sets of images are integrated by a continuous soundtrack. His best work of this kind is *Time Stepping* (1974) where two cameras play a rhythmic space–time game, shooting alternately and panning away in opposite directions down the street from the same central point, two doorways at the front of a row of old houses. The film from both cameras is edited together in the sequence and duration of its shooting, any gaps between the takes being represented by black spacing, and any overlap between the camera runs being represented by superimposition. A second section of the film maintains the parallel between projection and shooting durations. Whilst single frames from the camera are projected in the normal 1/24 second, from the other single-frame one-second time-exposures are stretch-printed to equal their original exposure time. This follows up the exploration of the single-frame time-exposure in another of his films, *Colours of this Time* (1972), where the colour temperature of the light at different times of the day is given its maximum effect on the film's colour emulsion by vastly increasing exposure time while diminishing the light intensity through a dense, neutral-toned filter.

Another identifiable sampling tendency has been that relating to spatial or rotational movements of the camera. A number of film-makers have independently explored the use of a controlled lateral movement of the camera in discrete units of time and degrees moved. Again, Chris

Wellsby, with *Fforest Bay II* (1972), contributed to this direction, as did John Ducane with *Together at Last* and *Pan Film* (both 1972); and, more recently, Heinz Emigholz with *Arrow Plane* (1973). All these films are concerned with changing spatial perception through progressively altering the rate of change of the image. In fact, much of the work involving systemic structures has, perhaps unconsciously, involved an almost mathematical process of stabilizing certain variables, whilst others are shifted, showing correlations rarely noticed in films concerned with subjective response and expression. All the above films in some way explore the concept of sampling from the panning action of the camera. In each, when time compression results in a rapid apparent motion, then the rate of change in the images begins to visibly deform the space being recorded.

Transformation of spatial experience in this way can be seen as a more general issue. In some works by Brakhage, like *Sirius Remembered*, and others influenced by his camera movement, there is often the effect of flattening the image on the screen, due to the blur of a rapid pan. In the opening sequence of Ruttmann's *Berlin* the images shot from a fast-moving train become similarly flattened and abstracted; however, the first film to display a clear awareness of the spatial implications of camera movement and velocity is Michael Snow's ←→ (1969). In this film the periods of rapid panning, both sideways and up and down, flatten the space in the pictorially abstract sense. But, as in Kren's *Bäume im Herbst*, Snow's use of the camera is a fairly direct parallel to Cézanne's basic discovery that the perception and conception of space and spatial relationships are a product of the observational procedure. Like Cézanne, they do not transform a 'real' deep space into a pictorial shallow space, but overthrow an existing convention of perspective. Perspective embodies in plastic terms a particular conception of the human condition. An ineffective relationship to nature is expressed through deep space, and the psychologically 'distanced', immobile viewpoint.

Together with Kren's *Bäume im Herbst*, Snow's ←→ establishes the interdependence of the viewpoint or process of observation and the thing observed in modern cinematic form. However, Snow's film also contexts perceptions of space by tracing a range of transformations throughout the film: from the conventional perspective space of the static camera, passing through camera movements which seem to 'stretch' the width of the screen beyond Cinemascope, or alternatively compress the two ends of the room into the short screen width, finally reaching the point where the image is a blur of sheer screen or emulsion surface. In this film, the spectacular transformations are seen as a result of camera velocity, though from films which have followed ←→ it begins to be evident that velocity is not the only factor in its relativistic conception of film space and film time. It should be said that this aspect of the film, whilst being its major 'content', is somewhat diminished, as in *Wavelength*, by the attempted exercise of various literary, narrative devices, overstretching the 'integrity' of the film. However, the camera aspect of the film has been directly influential and is a point of reference for many subsequent developments.

Though there are other roots, the systemic camera work described must be seen in relationship to ←→ and in some cases as a development

Michael Snow: ←→, 1969

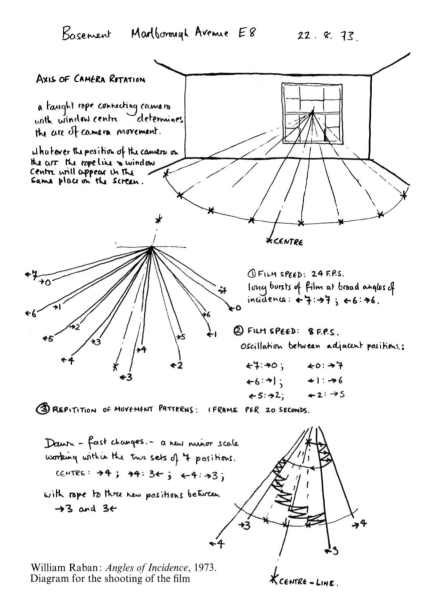

William Raban: *Angles of Incidence*, 1973.
Diagram for the shooting of the film

from it. Stretching an historical parallel, where ⟷ and *Bäume im Herbst* relate to the innovation in painting by Cézanne, some subsequent developments in cinema where the camera itself moves through space in a controlled and graspable pattern relate to the shifting viewpoint of Cubism. This is supported by Raban's *Angles of Incidence* (1973). Very related to the panning films, this is significantly different in its spatial implications. In this film, the camera, instead of panning on its tripod head, is actually shifted in measured units around a semi-circular arc, always keeping the centre of a window at the same distance, and in the centre of the frame. The shooting system is similar to the pan-rotation films of Ducane, Wellsby or Emigholz, taking certain numbers of frames within a controlled angular movement. However, the spatial movement of the observational point itself, compressed in time through the projection, creates a filmic equivalent to Cubist space. Another film which has a similar result is *Double Shutter* (1971) by Dutchman Mattijn Seip, where the camera is mounted on a swing, moving in an arc, in and out of the space which it observes. In this film, the camera also has a secondary shutter mounted before the lens, rotating at various speeds and interacting with the shutter of the camera as it also explores different running speeds. In both films, the objects often take on 'distortions' very similar to the actual shapes in Cubist painting. Surface similarities in shape, however, are not the main basis of the parallel with Cubism; most important is the way in which the spatial construct of the film is a product of the relationship of the space of the camera to the space which it observes.

Snow himself represents this development with a high degree of clarity in *The Central Region*. This extremely long film, shot from a hilltop in a barren landscape, makes use of a complex mechanical tripod able to rotate the camera in any direction at a great variety of speeds. Though the images which result from this mechanism do not resemble Cubist forms, the conceptual structure of the film's time–space is related to a classical Cubist procedure. The concept of space can be seen as an interaction between the elements existing in the space, and the trajectory and velocity of that which observes or explores it.

The films of Snow, and the other work based on the camera function, lead to some general questions about film structure. In *Wavelength* the component events are co-ordinated by a predetermined filmic shape. In ←→, whilst there is the remnant of a similar predeterminate form for the whole film, much of the 'content' is the result of a unifying camera strategy. For Snow, this method is brought to a peak in the programmed machine which controlled the camera in *The Central Region*. Though Snow's film is 'procedural', 'systemic' works like *Fforest Bay* by Wellsby are also structured by a fixed strategy rather than a predetermined holistic shape. However, in the systemic films, the determinate quality of the system can lead to a false assumption that all 'content' is controlled by the system. In fact, many assumptions condition the form of the system and how and where it should be applied, and these are as much a source of subjective 'content' as the choice of symbols in a Symbolist work. Determinate systems may create the illusion of eliminating 'subjective' choice whilst all they do is shift the region in which it operates.

It is a recognition of this which has led to more complex notions of procedural determinants which may not be mathematical, mechanistic or strictly predeterminate. This shift from the systemic to the more responsively procedural is seen for example in Raban's *Time Stepping*. The complexity of the inter-relationship between predetermined strategy, specific limitations and resultant film structure is specifically taken on by Roger Hammond in his *Ehrlanger Programme* (1971) and *Some Friends* (1973), and by Gidal with great consistency in *Bedroom* (1971), *Room Film 1973* (1973) and *Film Print* (1974). I will take up the Hammond films later in relationship to other questions of film structure because they are less directly related to the camera issue.

Gidal's major contribution comes in his concentration on issues of structuring directly related to the act of perceiving through the camera and the projection of the film. His work in this area represents a complex dialectic between subjective existential response on the one hand, and a reflexive structural concept on the other. His work is procedural in the sense of establishing specific limitations to his action, like the length of film in the camera, the space in which he will work (repeatedly a single room), and the objects which will occupy the space.

His work does not deny his own response to light, surface, or the identity of the object, but it contexts this subjectivity within the recognizable limits of the process. In fact, his handling of the camera, framing, focus and zoom are clearly apparent, indicating his moment-to-moment response to the visual field. However he is not aiming to reconstruct his own motives for the viewer, but to alert them to their reflexive attention in relationship to the 'events' which occur before them on the screen. Such systemic devices which Gidal has used, as in *Room Film 1973* where 100-foot continuous takes are broken down into equal five-second units and each one shown twice, maintaining their original sequence, are concerned with the act of perception, and its various stages of recognition and conception. In it the perceptual stages are deliberately prolonged—an indistinct region of light on the screen will become more distinctly a surface, though not clearly the surface of an object. Then it may take on an edge, but the scale has to be guessed at, being gradually confirmed, denied or neither by the film's subsequent progress. Then it may or may not become recognizable as a book or a shelf, only for the camera to move on to another region—every stage being drawn out by the sometimes nearly indecipherable double view of each segment. Experiences which in our everyday perception are over in an unconscious flash, in Gidal's films become extended processes for conscious attention and structuring.

Unlike other film-makers who have been concerned with a reflexive mode for the audience, Gidal, except perhaps in *Hall*, has never elicited it by the kind of puzzle-game used in Frampton's *Zorns Lemma*. His films have always maintained a distinct link between the act of perception, conception and realization available through viewing the film, and the act of perception and definition of time, space, surface, material and object available through the use of a movie camera. Other film-makers share some of Gidal's reflexive, structural intentions, to whom I shall refer anon, but for the moment I shall continue to consider developments which spring from a concern with the camera event.

Recently a number of works directly referential to the camera and its functioning have been produced. This development can be seen as part of a general tendency towards a conceptual approach to the processes of filming and projection. Of those films which refer directly to the camera within the work, the most interesting have been by Raban, Gidal, David Crosswaite, Gill Eatherley and Mike Dunford. I have already discussed Raban's *Soft Edge* and *Time Stepping*, but this direction first emerged clearly in Gidal's *Movie No. 1* (1972), where a narrator blandly describes the correlation between film exposure, the rate of motion within the image and the camera's running speed. This is visually demonstrated in two situations, one with a static camera and a hand switching a table light repeatedly on and off, the second with a hand-held camera viewing

Peter Gidal: *Room Film 1973*, 1973

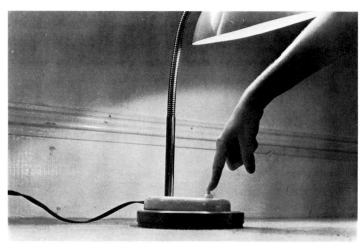

Peter Gidal: *Movie No. 1*, 1972

David Crosswaite: *Man with the Movie Camera*, 1973

a photograph on a wall.

Crosswaite's *Man with the Movie Camera* (1973) is a particularly elegant film. By mounting a circular mirror a little before the camera, so that it only occupies the central area of the screen, and another mirror to the side, the camera and its cameraman may be seen as the central image, with the other features of the room visible around the circumference. The film is complex in spite of the simplicity of the set-up which is only slowly grasped. Particularly succinct is the way in which the effect of manipulating the camera, like changing focus, is seen in the image simultaneously with a view of how it is brought about. There is no other 'content' than the functioning of the camera itself, seen to be sufficient and even poetic.

In Gill Eatherley's *Dialogue* (1973), two cameras are used to explore the view from a window and then within a room, the camera operators closely follow and complement each other, even frequently observing each other directly. The film traces the two cameras' attempts to imitate each other's action—thus making some of the subjective responses of camera handling more explicit.

A similar intention lies behind some of the recent works of Dunford, *Still Life* (1973), *Deep Space* (1973) and *Arbitrary Limits* (1974). In *Still Life*, movement of the camera around a clearly contrived and strongly lit bowl of fruit is accompanied by a soundtrack giving instructions for the movement, sometimes preceding, sometimes following it. In *Deep Space*, three sections of the film, shot from the same place in a London street, explore distinctly different modes of camera use—the first static on a tripod, the second steady but hand-held, and the third, in violent motion. The fourth section of the film involves a single-frame freeze from the third section of filming. In *Arbitrary Limits* the action of the camera is determined by the physical problem of holding it, unsupported, at arm's length, movements being directly related to muscular fatigue. The soundtrack records the film-maker's comments as he struggles to maintain the position and steadiness of the camera.

Mike Dunford: *Arbitrary Limits*, 1974. Polaroid of the film-maker shooting the film

In all these films, the action of the camera, its mechanisms and handling are deliberately isolated as a conceptual element in the work. A number of other film-makers have also contributed to this direction in

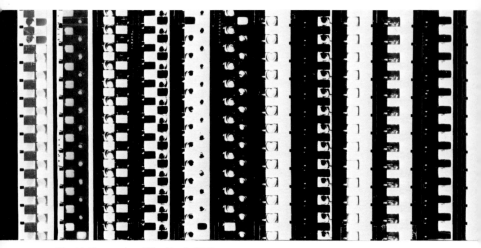

David Crosswaite: *Film No. 1*, 1969

one form or another, particularly Renny Croft, Morgan Fisher, David Dye and Tim Head.

The next area to consider is that which is concerned with post-camera structuring. Again the range is wide, including systemic editing, as in Bill Brand's *Moment* (1972), systemic procedure in printing as in Mike Leggett's *Shepherd's Bush* (1971), and systematic restructuring through refilming from the screen as in John Ducane's *Sign* (1973). It also includes reflexive modes from the deterministic puzzle of Frampton's *Zorns Lemma* (1970), to the provocative tract of Landow's *Institutional Quality* (1969), and the procedurally reflexive work of Gidal and Hammond. In many respects, the historical roots for the systemic approach to editing can be found in Kren's early work, as the reflexive aspect of systemic structure is also first seen in his *TV* of 1968. The systemic or permutative aspects of printing are probably initiated by my own *Reign of the Vampire* (1969) or Crosswaite's *Film No. 1* of the same year.

The roots of the less systemic aspects of reflexive intention are much more difficult to pin down, or even define. Much European work since 1966, particularly that by Kren, the Heins, Weibel, Gidal and myself, has been expressly concerned with eliciting an active, structuring mode in the audience. In America since that time, Snow, Landow, Sharits,

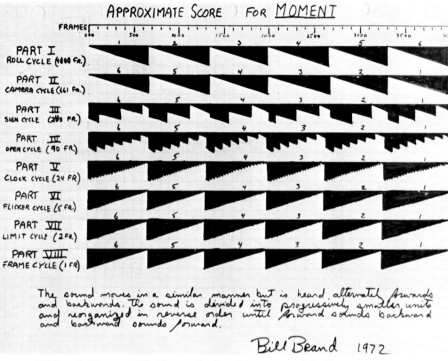

Bill Brand: *Moment*, 1972. Diagram for the editing system of the film

Frampton and, in some works, Jacobs, seem to have had similar intentions, though concern with the mode of audience reaction and perception seems only to have been expressed directly in the theoretical writing of European film-makers, frequently viewed as a political as well as an aesthetic issue. This can be seen as a development of Vertov's stance—a politics of perception.

It is in eliciting a conscious, structuring mode in the audience that the systemic direction has most validity, though this can lead to a deterministic form where the mode is simply one of unravelling the nature of the film-maker's particular 'scrambler'. In this case, system tends to replace narrative as an 'involving' device. The most extreme pole of this quasi-reflexive use of systemic editing is represented by Bill Brand's *Moment*, where the system is a strict programme. In this film, a single, two-and-a-half minute continuous shot is edited through a series of fragmentations. Progressively presented in reverse order to their shooting, it ends in a total, frame-by-frame reversal of the original sequence. Some of the determinism of the work is salvaged by an appropriate choice of image, a view of a garage through a rotating slat advertisement, whose physical structure is a direct parallel for the kind of 'slatting' system applied to the film.

The best examples of systemic structure which derives from printing are extensions of the loop-printing concept. With loops of film as the basis, permutative relationships between loops of different kinds or lengths can often be followed through more simply than where material is edited according to system. Again, the problem of narrow determinism applies to work of this kind, the most interesting work not necessarily being defined by the nature of the system applied. Crosswaite's *Film No. 1* explores a simple permutation of travelling-matte loops. The original material of this film is unsplit 8mm film, which results in four images being projected simultaneously when shown in 16mm. The film is printed so that each of the four very simple images changes independently, building up a pattern of rhythmic interchange. As in my loop-permutated *Reign of the Vampire*, appreciation of the system is kinetic and perceptual rather than intellectual, neither film encourages any kind of 'puzzling' out of the system, though it is plain that the film's repetitions have a systemic pattern.

Similarly, the system is not a 'content' to be 'discovered' in Leggett's *Shepherd's Bush*. A loop of film shot from a fast-moving camera, presumably close to the ground, is repeatedly printed, each time with a change in the exposure, so that its visual quality alters in imperceptible stages from totally black to totally white, while the soundtrack, also a continuously repeated pattern, gets lower and lower in pitch. The systemic or structural aspect of this film is again partly directed towards the appreciation of duration through attention to minimal developments in the image.

Since Jacobs' *Tom Tom the Piper's Son* (1969), and the Heins' *Grün*, a number of film-makers have used refilming from the screen as a means of transforming the image, particularly extending the time of a sequence or exploiting the changes in visual qualities of lighting, resolution and grain as in work by Ernie Gehr. One of the most interesting films of this kind is David Rimmer's *Surfacing on the Thames* (1970), where a very short sequence of a steam-boat passing down the river is extended to eight minutes by attention to each frame of the film, especially its surface qualities of grain and scratches. Refilming is controlled to the extent of shifting focus through the film strip, from the surface qualities on one side to the surface qualities on the other. Ducane has also made a number of films which begin from a sequence of film shot often in single frames or with a fast-moving camera, then, as in *Sign*, the original material is refilmed from the screen progressively allowing longer and longer attention to the component frames as the sequence is repeated; or, as in *Praxi* (1974), reordering the sequence of shots, like shuffling a pack of cards. A different use of refilming from the screen is not concerned with transforming the image, but is a reference to the act of filming and its relationship to the act of projection, to which I shall return.

Mike Leggett: *Shepherd's Bush*, 1971

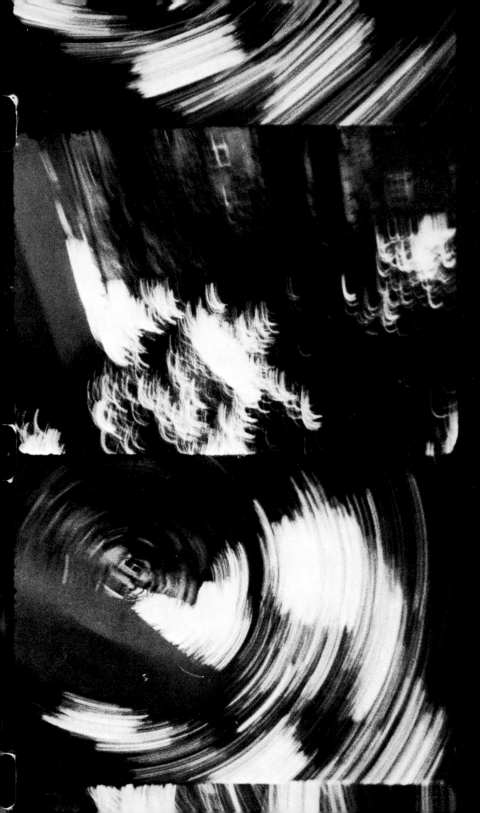

to pupil is an emo

George Landow: *Remedial Reading Comprehension*, 1970

*left*
John Ducane: *Sign*, 1973

In discussing Gidal's *Room Film 1973* I considered the reflexive activity in relationship to a continuous act of perceiving, defining and structuring. For the audience, a process of assessment and prediction seems to be essential to a reflexive concept of cinema. The simplest form of this emerges in the puzzle format, as in Frampton's *Zorns Lemma*, where he exchanges sequences of words arranged in alphabetical order for twenty-four 'action' sequences. Though the film has many levels of aesthetic control, and the nuances of the 'game' are varied, the general implication of the form for the audience is that there is a solution to be worked out, existing, as it were, *a priori* in the work. This conditions the nature of the reflexive behaviour which the audience engages in. A less deterministic mode is brought about in Frampton's more recent *Poetic Justice* (1972), where the film image is no more than the sequential presentation of sheets of a film script, written to demand a conscious structuring or corrected restructuring of the events described in the script with careful, deliberate ambiguity.

In Landow's *Institutional Quality* and *Remedial Reading Comprehension* (1970), the reflexive mode takes on a provocative function. By addressing the audience directly through the film, giving instructions, asking questions or proclaiming blandly 'this is a film about you—not about its maker', it forces the audience to recognize that apparent surface intentions, like the instructions to participate in a way which

139

Gill Eatherley: *Pan Film*, 1971, showing layout of three-screen projection

particular problem selected for attention is only one aspect of the wider meaning of the work. It is a project towards extending clarity about the material and perceptual phenomena of film, but one which realizes the continuing development of the phenomena being studied. The work is perhaps as significant for the 'long-term' attitude which it embodies as for the specific films.

The next and very evident current, major development stems from a concern with projection. Within this there are three well defined though interacting areas: the extension of multi-projection forms, film-based actions or performances and installations. Abel Gance's three-screen *Napoleon* of 1927 can be seen at least as a symbolic beginning for this aspect of cinema, but in fact the multi-media combination of film projection, light machines, music and performance was an aspect of the Bauhaus in the early twenties, pioneered by Moholy-Nagy, Hirschfeld-Mack, Josef Hartwig and Kurt Schwerdtfeger.

The formal direction in this area, as it has emerged in Europe, is not relatable to the psychedelic tendency of American expanded cinema seen in the Vortex concerts of the late fifties, and the multi-projection work by Stan Vanderbeek in the sixties. The initial impetus for the current developments came mainly from Weibel, Export, and myself, all three continuing to work in this area, though most of Weibel's recent work is in video rather than film. One or two other film-makers, like Mommartz, Nekes and Drummond, made some double-projection work around 1969, but have not followed this up. Whilst Weibel and Export have largely concentrated on performance or lecture formats, my own work represents the most consistent exploration of the possibilities of formal multi-projection. However, in the last two or three years a number of other film-makers have become deeply involved in these directions, particularly in Britain, and the range of experiment is now extremely wide.

My use of multi-projection until 1971 was largely designed to allow comparison between two screens. Extending to a third screen in some cases, the simultaneous presentation is used for comparison of different printings or organizations of the same basic material, as in *Berlin Horse* (1970) and *1919, A Russian Funeral* (1971). This direction has also been

142

taken by Gill Eatherley, a prolific young film-maker whose work since her first film in 1972 has already passed through a number of stages. Her first films, like *Shot Spread* (1972) and particularly *Pan Film* (1971), isolate and concentrate on more basic aspects of the comparative function. *Pan Film* is an extremely simple, short film in two- and three-screen versions, composed of a number of short, slow pans across a room, past a partially open window that gives only a glimpse of the trees outside. Its presentation on two or three screens is concerned to develop an experience of basic factors of film's topology—reversal of the lateral axis which changes the direction of the pans, and reversal of the tonal distribution through use of negative and positive copies. The four versions of the original shots made possible by the combination of these topological transformations are then presented in various relationships with each other. This creates a film where negative and positive sequences pan slowly, either in the same direction or counter to each other. A by-product of the work's simplicity is an awareness of the way in which the camera motion, and its effect on space, is altered significantly when presented in the comparative format. This is an area with new and interesting problems which she has since taken up in *Doubles Round* (1973).

The major extension of formal multi-projection has come in one way or another through treating projection as the primary area of film's 'reality'. For the film's audience, the only point of contact with cinema as a material reality comes through the actual time and space of projection. Film, as a photographic medium, presents to the audience an illusion of a time and space normally quite unrelatable to the time and space which they actually occupy whilst watching the film.

Where Warhol created a near one-to-one correspondence between the camera event and the projection event, projection remained a secondary consequence. Recent work, concentrating on the projection event itself, has attempted to reverse this assumption by establishing the primacy of the situation in which the audience has access to the work. This can also be interpreted philosophically as an attempt to establish for the film audience the primacy of current experience over the illusory or retrospective, and is consistent with the 'material' preoccupation of

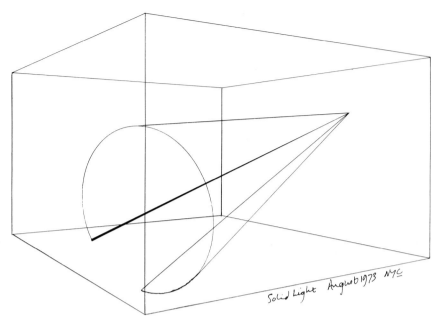

Anthony McCall: *Line Describing a Cone*, 1973. Diagram of the projection
concept

modern avant-garde film. From this position, two directions affecting
both multi-projection and performance/projection events can be broadly
defined, again as two 'poles' rather than distinct categories.

On the one hand, there is the attempt to eliminate or diminish the
retrospective aspect, dealing only with the physical elements actually
present in the projection situation. This has led to a number of recent
works by Carolee Schneemann and Valie Export, for example, where
there is a clear overlap with some elements of 'body art', often dispensing
with film completely. On the other hand, there is a direction which
attempts to incorporate the retrospective, photographic aspect of cinema,
structuring it to be directly relatable to the primary event of projection.

Not all the work which focusses on the projection event involves
multi-projection or performance. One example of such work, which at
the same time represents an extreme pole in the establishment of the
'concrete' and non-retrospective aspect of projection, is Anthony
McCall's *Line Describing a Cone* (1973), in which there should be no
screen. Instead the image is three-dimensional, contained in the light-
beam from the projector itself. A point of light from the black film, when
viewed from beside the projector beam, is seen as a line, in space,
running outwards from the projector lens. During thirty minutes the
point on the film surface extends to become the circumference of a

144

circle, so that the line from the projector consequently describes the surface of a cone—a time sculpture using 'solid' light. Perhaps his work represents the real progression from the early abstract cinema of Eggeling. The other pole is largely initiated by the early works of Export, like *Ping Pong*.

David Dye has also contributed to the attempt to establish clear parallels between the conditions of the projection event and the retrospective aspect of the film's shooting, and has produced a number of pieces which create a direct analogue between the camera and the projector. Working in 8mm or super 8, he has frequently made film 'pieces' where the projector is actually handled in the same way as a camera, using zoom focus and moving the frame. For example, one piece from 1970 involves projection onto a sheet of canvas, behind which is a small portable projection screen, obscured except for the top left-hand corner. The projector, hand-held with only a small image size, travels around the perimeter of the canvas, showing a film of the screen hidden directly beneath. In another piece from the same year, *Confine* (1970), a photograph on a wall is filmed whilst walking away from it, the picture getting progressively smaller in the frame. This is then projected, again with a hand-held projector, attempting to keep the image of the photograph exactly within a tape rectangle on the projection screen, causing the projector to repeat the path and motion of the camera.

David Dye: *Confine*, 1970. Photograph of projection performance

explains that a film is being made of the screen, and a recording made of the sound, including that of the audience. This 100 feet of film (2 minutes 45 seconds long) is processed by the film-maker in a small tank, ready for the next stage of the piece, normally the following day. In the second stage, this negative film of the first stage replaces the blank screen, and the first sound recording is replayed. The film-maker again announces the nature of the work on the second performance, which is similarly filmed and recorded. That version is then developed and presented at the next performance, and so on. The various stages of the film recede screen within screen, moving from negative to positive on successive shows, creating a space illusion as a time analogue.

Conrad's untitled feedback film is very similar in appearance to that of Raban's, but is the result of an unbroken film-feedback cycle. Film is run continuously from a camera to a hand-developing, fixing and drying system. From there it is fed directly into a projector, the image cast onto the screen, and immediately refilmed by the camera, and so on. The only image other than the screen itself is a candle in front of the camera which slowly burns down showing the unbroken continuity of the action. As in Raban's film, the screens recede in an interchanging negative–positive time-corridor, extending in depth with each successive stage.

Recently, a number of film-makers, like Eatherley, Crosswaite and myself, but chiefly Sharits, Iimura and Conrad, have experimented with continuously running film installations or static film displays. In the case of the British work, like Eatherley's *Chair Installation*, my own *Gross Fog* and Crosswaite's *Thames Studio*—all of 1973—these have mainly been multi-projection pieces which have little change in time, and can be presented for an indeterminate period. With Sharits, it is an attempted solution to the problem of showing work within the context of an art gallery as in the plexi-glass installations like *Frozen Film Frame* (1973) (see illustration page 151) or his use of three- or four-loop projectors arranged to form a composite image, usually based on the simulation of a single three- or four-frame segment of an actual film strip.

Both Conrad and Iimura have experimented with film installation in terms of extensive duration, utilizing forms which show loops for very long periods of time. One of Iimura's installations is conceived as an extremely long contemplation of the gradual deterioration in long loops of clear black film. Conrad's concern began with the durational aspect of *The Flicker* and his long period of involvement with the musician La Monte Young. His untitled loop installation of slightly shifting vertical stripes (1972) is concerned with the meditative aspect of extensive repetition, but his most significant and challenging contribution in this area comes with his *Yellow Movies* series (1973), which are not projected works but large sheets of paper in the common film-screen proportions, each painted a single colour ranging between white and yellow. The materials are 'specific', the paper and paint being named together with the dimensions, within the title-description of each work. The duration is also 'specific', being the period from the initial date of the work to the date on which it is currently being viewed.

Some of Conrad's and Iimura's recent work does not easily relate to the areas I have defined. Conrad's is a provocative extension of the hand-made, material aspect of film, with some curious similarities to the

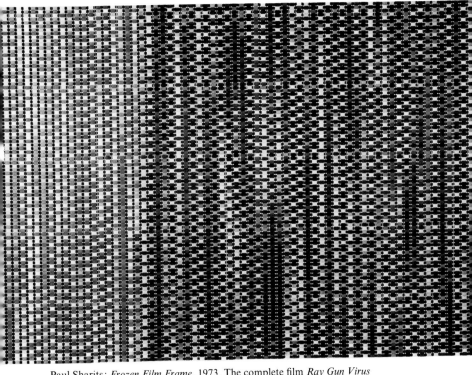

Paul Sharits: *Frozen Film Frame*, 1973. The complete film *Ray Gun Virus* displayed between plexi-glass sheets

qualities inherent in Nicolson's performances. He deliberately challenges assumptions about the film material, its chemical development and means of viewing, in a series of works which, for example, chemically 'develop' the film in food-based recipes like curry, or pickle it like onions in vinegar and spice. The resultant works are either difficult or impossible to project, as in the case of the film deep-fried in cooking oil which is too brittle even to be lifted from its film can.

Iimura has entered a highly conceptual area of cinematic duration, incidentally using another development from the hand-made film. Much of his work of 1973 and 1974 has been based on the act of counting or measuring time in stable intervals. Using the consistency of projection speed, and the simple method of marking in felt-tipped pen directly onto film stock, his works concentrate entirely on ranges of time-interval. They can also be thought of within the sense of research or film exercise, as their intention is no more and no less than a detailed examination of our perceptual and conceptual mechanisms in relationship to time-intervals.

One of these works begins with a series of very simple mathematical equations, whose parts are expressed by lengths of blank black or white film. Two film-strips are 'added' together to produce a third equal in duration to the sum of the two strips previously seen. However, when 'subtracting' instead of 'adding', the film-strips, still moving forward in time, 'subtract' from each other to produce a shortened third. The effect produced by applying the idea of subtraction to material duration is a surprisingly strong experience of negative duration—backward-running time. This is an interesting example of how new form creates new thought and experience; indeed how innovation in form is a pre-requisite for innovation in thought.

The innovations in film form outlined in this book represent the most important creative extension in the history of film thought. Film has moved progressively towards a form which is not dependent on other areas of art for the source of its conventions, not only breaking the stranglehold of theatre and literature, but also developing past the alternative dependence on painting and music. Since the war we have seen the gradual emergence of a film art which is genuinely cinemato-graphic in concept. While no conclusions can be drawn about the most recent work—in that respect this chapter should finish symbolically in mid-sentence—and though this form of cinema becomes more wide-spread, it is still underpinned by a view of film, its conventions, language and social relationship in almost direct opposition to the dominant popular cinema culture.

Many film-makers who have contributed to the abstract or formal avant-garde cinema have recognized this opposition as a political problem. Statements which I have quoted by the Futurists, Léger and Vertov confirm this. Because my main concern with the modern move-ment has been to trace the aesthetic and formal developments, I have largely ignored political argument. However, many of the film-makers, like the Heins, Weibel, Gidal and myself have written about this problem. The political questions of formal cinema centre, not on the issue of political content in the films, but on the political implications of the film's language, conventions and structure. Most importantly formal cinema centres on the mode of perception and conception which is available to the viewer of the film. Form determines the mode of response in the audience. It is in this respect that I will risk some generalizations about aims implicit in the whole historical development of abstract and formal cinema.

Firstly it seeks to be 'realist' in the material sense. It does not imitate or represent reality, nor create spurious illusions of times, places and lives which engage the spectator in a vicarious substitute for his own reality. To this end, film-makers have paid increasing attention to the actuality of their materials and processes. Parallel to other areas of twentieth-century art (though not at all mainstream cinema), they have gone a long way towards establishing a concept of cinema with its base in the material aspects of the medium. From this basis, they have come to realize the extending complexity of this enterprise, for to create a material basis for art is no simple programme. It encounters the problem of inevitable subjectivity: however much the work of art is a 'phenom-enon' for the spectator, it still has a maker who is constrained within both physical and historical limits, in particular, within the conventions which currently exist in his medium.

So, secondly, the abstract and formal cinema seeks clarification within the films themselves of the relationship between the subjectivity of the film-maker, the constraints of his 'language' and the subjectivity of the film-viewer. The search for this clarity of means, coupled with the attempt to give to the spectator an affirmation of his own reality has led to the emergence of deliberately reflexive forms. Thirdly, therefore, it seeks to counteract the emotional manipulation and reactionary catharsis of popular cinematic form by the development of conscious, conceptual and reflexive modes of perception thus representing the most advanced and radical state of cinematic language and convention.

Gill Eatherley: Chair Installation, 1973. Photograph of a film-slide and shadow installation

# Notes

CHAPTER 1

1 From *Futurist Manifestos*, ed. Umbro Apollonio.
2 To date the most informative research available into these films is contained in Michael Kirby's *Futurist Performance*.


CHAPTER 2

1 From *Futurist Manifestos*. 'Abstract Cinema—Chromatic Music' was published originally as part of a collection of critical articles by Corra and Settimelli (*Il pastore, il gregge e la zampogna*, Libreria Beltrami).
2 From *Futurist Manifestos*. For futher information see Scheugl and Schmidt, 'Lexicon des Avant-garde-Experimental-Underground Films', *Bianco e Nero*, 10–12 (1967).
3 From 'The Film as an Original Art Form', *Film Culture*, Vol. 1 no. 1 (January 1955).
4 In *Hans Richter*.
5 From an article in *De Stijl* (10 May 1921).
6 In *Das Kunstblatt*, Vol. 8, Berlin (1924).
7 In *Hans Richter*.
8 From an article in *Experiment in the Film*, ed. Roger Manvell.
9 Much of my information on Fischinger draws heavily on the work of Elfriede Fischinger and William Moritz, kindly made available to me before its publication. This work should sort out many of the chronological uncertainties as Fischinger was a careful collector of documents.


CHAPTER 3

1 In *Little Review*, (Winter 1926). Reprinted in *Introduction to the Art of the Movies* compiled by Lewis Jacobs.
2 From an article in *Studio International*, Vol. 189 no. 973 (January–February 1975).


CHAPTER 4

1 From an article in *Experiment in the Film*, ed. Roger Manvell.
2 In *Hans Richter*.


CHAPTER 5

1 Translated by Christoph Giercke in *Afterimage*, no. 1.
2 From *Cinema in Revolution*, ed. Luda Schnitzer et al.
3 From *Afterimage*, no. 1.
4 From 'Leninist proportion' by Seth Feldman, *Sight and Sound* (Winter 1973/4).
5 From *Afterimage*, no. 1.

CHAPTER 6

1 The film has only recently been discovered, and I have had no opportunity to see it, but by William Moritz's description, it must be considered an important work.

CHAPTER 7

1 In *Expanded Cinema*.
2 See *Film Culture*, no. 37 (Summer 1965).
3 With Austin Lamont in *Film Comment* (Fall 1970).
4 In *Expanded Cinema*.

CHAPTER 8

1 In *Film Culture*, No. 47 (Summer 1969).
2 In *Film Culture*, No. 29 (Summer 1973). A transcript from a symposium at Cinema 16, 28 October 1953.
3 In 'L'existentialisme est un humanisme', a lecture given in 1946, translated by Philip Mairet.
4 Roland Barthes, 'The Structuralist Activity', from *Essais Critiques*, Editions du Sequil, 1964. English translation by Richard Howard, *Partisan Review* (Winter 1967), Vol. 34 No. 1.
5 Ibid.

CHAPTER 9

1 From *Futurist Manifestos* ed. Umbro Apollonio.
2 In *Film im Underground*.

155

# Selected bibliography

BOOKS

Apollonio, Umbro (ed.): *Futurist Manifestos.* DuMont Schauberg, Cologne, 1970; Gabriele Mazzotta, Milan, 1970; Thames and Hudson, London, 1973; Viking Press, New York, 1973

Cawkwell, Tim and Smith, John M. (eds): *The World Encyclopedia of Film.* Studio Vista, London, 1972; A & W Visual Services, New York, 1975.

Curtis, David: *Experimental Cinema.* Studio Vista, London, 1971; Universe Books, New York, 1971

Eisenstein, Sergei M.: *Film Form* (trans. Jay Leyda). Dobson, London, 1951; Harcourt Brace Jovanovich, New York, 1969.

——*Film Sense* (trans. Jay Leyda). Faber and Faber, London, 1969; Harcourt Brace Jovanovich, New York, 1969.

Geduld, Harry M. (ed.): *Film Makers on Film Making.* Penguin Books, London, 1967; Indiana University Press, 1967.

Gidal, Peter: *Andy Warhol.* Studio Vista, London, 1971; Dutton, New York, 1971.

—— (ed.) *Structural Film Anthology*, BFI, London, 1976

Graham, Peter: *A Dictionary of the Cinema.* Zwemmer, London, 1968; A. S. Barnes, New York, 1968.

Hein, Birgit: *Film im Underground.* Ulstein, Frankfurt-Berlin-Vienna, 1971.

——& Wilhelm: *X Screen* (ed. Christian Michelis and Rolf Wiest). Phaidon, Cologne, 1971.

Jacobs, Lewis (ed.): *Introduction to the Art of the Movies.* Noonday, New York, 1960.

Kandinsky, Wassily: *Concerning the Spiritual in Art.* First published Germany, 1912; Wittenborn, New York, 1966.

Kirby, Michael: *Futurist Performance.* Dutton, New York, 1971.

Kracauer, Siegfried: *From Caligari to Hitler.* Oxford University Press, 1967; Princeton University Press, 1969.

Leyda, Jay: *Kino.* Allen and Unwin, 1960; Macmillan, New York, 1971.

Lipton, Lenny: *Independent Filmmaking.* Studio Vista, London, 1974; Straight Arrow Books, San Francisco, 1972.

MacCann, Richard Dyer (ed.): *Film: A Montage of Theories.* Dutton, New York, 1966.

Manvell, Roger (ed.): *Experiment in the Film.* Grey Walls Press, London, 1949; Arno Press & The New York Times, New York, 1970.

Moholy-Nagy, Laszlo: *Painting, Photography, Film.* First published in the Bauhausbücher series, no. 8, 1925; trans. J. Seligman, Lund Humphries, London and Bradford, 1969; MIT Press, Cambridge, Massachusetts, 1969.

Newhall, Beaumont: *The History of Photography.* Secker and Warburg, London, 1973; The Museum of Modern Art, New York, 1972.

O'Konor, Louise: *Viking Eggeling.* Almqvist & Wiksell, Stockholm, 1971.

Renan, Sheldon: *The Underground Film.* Studio Vista, London, 1968; Dutton, New York, 1967.

Richter, Hans: *Dada: Art and Anti-Art*. Thames and Hudson, London 1966; Abrams, New York, 1970.
——*Hans Richter* (ed. Cleve Gray). Thames and Hudson, London, 1971; Holt, Rinehart and Winston, New York, 1971.
Rotha, Paul: *The Film Till Now*. First published by Jonathan Cape, London, 1930; Spring Books, London, 1967; Twayne, New York.
Schamoni, Victor: *Das Lichtspiel, Möglichkeiten des Absoluten Films*. Druck Reimann, Hamburg, 1936.
Scheugl, Hans and Schmidt jnr, Ernst: *Eine Subgeschichte des Films, Lexikon des Avantgarde-Experimental-Undergroundfilms*. (2 vols). Edition Suhrkamp, Frankfurt am Main, 1974.
Schnitzer, Luda and Jean, and Martin, Marcel (eds): *Cinema in Revolution*. First published in French as *Le Cinéma Soviétique par ceux qui l'ont fait* by Les Editeurs Francais Reunis, Paris, 1966; Secker and Warburg, London, 1973; Hill and Wang, New York, 1973.
Sitney, P. Adams (ed.): *Film Culture*. Secker and Warburg, London, 1971; Praegar, New York, 1970.
——*Visionary Film*. Oxford University Press, New York, 1974.
Spottiswoode, Raymond: *A Grammar of the Film*. Faber and Faber, London, 1950; University of California Press, 1950.
Tyler, Parker: *Underground Film*. Secker and Warburg, London, 1971; Grove Press, New York, 1969.
Waldberg, Patrick: *Surrealism*. Thames and Hudson, London, 1966; McGraw-Hill, New York, 1966.
Youngblood, Gene: *Expanded Cinema*. Studio Vista, London, 1971; Dutton, New York, 1970.

PERIODICALS

*Afterimage* (London) Nos. 1–4.
*Art and Artists* (London), particularly Vol. 7 No. 9; issue No. 81, December 1972.
*Artforum* (New York). Frequent articles on American avant-garde film. Special issues on film: September 1971, January 1973.
*Ark:* Journal of the Royal College of Art (London) No. 46, Spring 1970.
*Canyon Cinemanews:* Canyon Cinema Co-op newsletter (Berkeley, California).
*Cinema* (Cambridge, England) Nos. 1–9.
*Cinema Rising* (London) No. 1.
*Cinim* (London) Nos. 1–4.
*Film Comment* (USA) Fall 1970.
*Film Culture* (New York).
*Interfunktionen* (Cologne) No. 4, March 1970.
*L'Art Vivant* (Paris) No. 52, October 1974.
*Light* (London) No. 1, 1973.
*Magazin Kunst* (Germany) No. 41, 1971.
*Sight and Sound* (London) Vol. 16 No. 64, 1947; Vol. 43 No. 1, Winter 1973/4.
*Studio International* (London), particularly Vol. 187 No. 963, February 1974; Vol. 189 No. 973, January/February 1975.
*Supervisuel* (Zurich).
*Village Voice* (New York), weekly column by Jonas Mekas.

CATALOGUES

Hamburg Film Makers' Co-operative.
Hamburg Filmschau 1972.
International Festival of Avant-Garde Film, London 1973.
International Underground Film Festival, London 1970.
London Film Makers' Co-operative.
Los Angeles Filmmakers' Co-operative.
Museum of Modern Art, Film Catalogue (New York).
Neuer Osterreichischer Film (complete to 1969).
New Forms in Film (American only), Montreux 1974.
New York Film Makers' Co-operative.
Progressive Art Productions, Munich.
A Survey of the Avant Garde in Britain, Gallery House, London
    (Vol. 3), 1972.
Twenty Four Frames, London.

# Index

Figures in italics refer to page numbers of illustrations

159